The Black Protagonist in the Cuban Novel

THE BLACK PROTAGONIST
IN THE CUBAN NOVEL

by Pedro Barreda

Translated by Page Bancroft

The University of Massachusetts Press

Amherst, 1979

To Tamara and Phillip

Contents

Preface

Although the theme of this book may have some relation to the growing interest in the United States in the problems of the American black and in African studies, in fact I cannot remember when the idea first came to me—perhaps "de nación,"* as Unamuno said, with a special meaning, from the people of my country. It is something that was in me before I became conscious of it: a rich deposit that had been formed in my spirit by the very air of my land, even before I was aware of breathing that air. That is the deep motivation that led me to study the characterization of the black protagonist in the Cuban novel. Another reason for my interest is that little work has been done on that theme. Unlike Afro-Antillean poetry, for which excellent critical work exists, the black novel in Cuba has not often attracted the attention of scholars. That fact strengthened my personal interest in and my inclination to devote myself to that aspect of the Cuban novel.

I have not attempted an exhaustive work. Nevertheless, when I discuss the most representative novels in which the black is the central figure—from the beginnings of the abolitionist novel to the stories written by the Cuban avant-gardists—I propose to trace the evolutionary process of the literary vision of the black in more than a century of Cuban novelistic production. At the same time, the chronological limits of this book determine to a certain extent one of its purposes: to clarify the attitude toward the black as it was reflected in the evolution of literary characterizations previous to the political changes that began to take place in Cuban society in 1959.

*Unamuno used *nación* not only to mean *nation* but also and particularly in its relation to *nacer*, "to be born." Hence lineage, heritage, birthright are included in its connotations.

I use the term *black* in a very broad sense to include not only Africans and their direct descendants but also mulattoes (in the case of the latter, I do, however, take into consideration the mixture of bloodlines). And I have included Martín Morúa Delgado's novel *Sofía* in this study in spite of the fact that the protagonist is biologically white, because the social determinism that conditions her to the role of a mulatto makes her behave like a black.

My intention has been aesthetic but not aestheticist. It has seemed essential to examine the black protagonist as an integral part of the story. Hence, in order to understand and illuminate the authentic profile, the study begins with an analysis of the novel in which the black is a character. The results of this critical work have been set into the historicoliterary process, following a generational arrangement.

I have tried to place these Cuban literary generations in the context of the general movements observed in Spanish America. In addition, in order to show those readers unfamiliar with the history of Cuba the background of some of the elements reflected in the characterization process, I have deemed it appropriate to offer by way of introduction a historical synthesis of the origin, development, and characteristics of the slave system that incorporated the black into the demographic composition of the island.

It remains for me to express publicly my thanks to all those who have helped me in the production of this book, especially to Professors George O. Schanzer, State University of New York at Buffalo, and Sumner Greenfield, University of Massachusetts at Amherst, who read the original manuscript, improved it with their observations, and encouraged me to publish it; to Page Bancroft for the interest she showed in the making of the English version; and to my wife, Tamara, without whose material and moral support this undertaking would have been impossible. I also wish to thank the University of Massachusetts for the economic aid offered through the conferral on me of a Faculty Research Grant. To all those, my most sincere thanks.

The Black Protagonist in the Cuban Novel

Chapter One
Slavery: The Incorporation of the Black into Cuban Society

To understand the black and mulatto segment of Cuban society—and its literary expression—it will help to outline briefly the way this group became incorporated in the demographic makeup of the island. There is no longer any doubt that Cuba is a mulatto nation, and the Cuban is, if not biologically, at least psychologically a mulatto. In Cuba the mixing of blood has not been so thorough as in other parts of the Antilles or in Brazil, but it is clear that the coexistence of various races within reduced geographical limits has favored a cultural interchange and a consequent creation of syncretic forms that to date have found their best artistic expression in music. This chapter examines the manner in which the black was introduced into Cuban society—through the slave trade—in order later to sketch the presence and development of the black theme in Cuban literature and thereby provide a framework for studying the characterization of the black protagonist in the Cuban novel.

Nineteen years after the discovery of Cuba in 1511, the conquest and colonization of the island began. That year, Diego Velázquez came from Hispaniola with a force of 300 men, among whom was Hernando Cortes, future conqueror of Mexico. By 1515 seven cities had been established: Baracoa, the capital, Bayamo, Santiago de Cuba, Puerto Príncipe, Sancti Spiritus, Trinidad, and Havana. The Indo-Cubans of the Paleolithic culture, the Ciboney—and the Neolithic Taino—were soon to disappear. It was to replace these Indians in working the mines that the importation of slaves began.

The introduction of African slaves into the Americas dates from 1501. Blacks were numerous before 1511 in Hispaniola, where they set a poor example for the Indians, inciting them to rebellion and flight, according to documents of that period.[1] As for Cuba, José Antonio Saco states that the first blacks were brought to the island from Santo Domingo between 1512 and 1514, because they were "so much needed."[2] Saco's hypothesis has been proved by Ramiro Guerra, who cites "the first authentic document known relating to the introduction of African slaves": the Royal Cedula "expedited 19 June 1513, in Valladolid, by which Amador de Lares was authorized to transport four Negro slaves from Hispaniola to Cuba."[3]

In both legal procedure and common trade, the Spaniards assigned the black a status inferior to that of the Indian. Marriage between whites and blacks was not authorized, and anyone with African ancestry was not considered to be "of clean blood." Nevertheless, the law offered facilities for manumission, and the number of freed blacks "increased constantly as the time passed."[4] On the other hand, the slaves were "so much needed" that in 1523 Carlos V authorized bringing 300 Africans to the island,[5] as shown in the first census taken in Cuba in 1544 by the bishop of the island, Don Diego Sarmiento. The total population was around 2,000; Indians made up almost half that number, and the existence of 500 African slaves was recorded.[6]

The scanty resources of Cuba's mines soon became evident, and by 1550 it was clear that the economy of Cuba would depend on the exploitation of sugar cane. This exploitation needed hands, black slave hands. That year, the governor of the island, Gonzalo Pérez de Angulo, sent Charles V a memorandum in which he asked for aid in establishing sugar mills, insisting on the need for African slaves; "he didn't beat around the bush in showing himself to be affiliated with the school that didn't conceive of the existence of sugar mills without slaves."[7] Spain acceded to his desires, and the trade in human flesh became a preponderant factor in the economic life of the country.

Blacks were requested not only for sugar production but for works of urbanization and defense. With the arrival in Havana of Don Diego de Mazariegos as military governor of the island in March 1566, construction was begun on a system of fortification for the city. To carry out the construction of the castle, La Fuerza, he asked the crown to send Africans, he recruited mulattoes who were marauding in the interior of the island, and he required neighbors to lend him their slaves.[8]

In the second half of the sixteenth century, the number of Africans increased as the number of Indians diminished. The population of freed blacks was also growing, and they cooperated in the defense of the villages and worked small parcels of land producing root and green vegetables. In the cities they did manual work, and in Havana they were permitted to keep inns for ship passengers. The municipal ordinances of Alonso de Cáceres (1574) allowed freed Negroes—because of the services they rendered—to bear arms. But the social position of the black population was inferior to that of the whites. For example, in 1571, black women were not permitted to wear the same finery as white women, in order to prevent the leveling of social classes.[9]

Oppressed by such an unjust and cruel system, the African slave was nonetheless protected by certain royal dispositions and municipal ordinances. The slaveowner was obliged to respect the life of the slave; "he could not mutilate him in any way, he had to feed him, clothe him, lodge him, and treat him well." [10] Slaves could contract valid marriages, but their offspring remained slaves. Cáceres, in the municipal ordinances of 1574, prevented speculation in African flesh by effectively prohibiting the resale of slaves. Once brought to the island as a *bozal* (an unskilled person with little knowledge of Spanish), the African could not be resold at a higher price. Consequently, an owner lost money if he put a slave up for sale after he had become acclimated and had learned a trade or a certain task. As a result, a slave stayed with the same owner for a long time, and then relationships gradually became more humanized. In addition, the slave had the right to be sold to another person if his owner treated him cruelly.

When Portugal became part of Spain, Philip II frequently granted to Portuguese traders *asientos,* licenses to export Africans to the coasts of America. The most important slave trader of that period was Gómez Reynal, who in 1595 was given a license to transport 4,500 slaves a year for a period of nine years. With the slaves Cuba received, "the sugar industry was able to develop advantageously." [11] Although the first Cuban refineries had only about twenty slaves, growth of the black population kept pace with the growth in sugar production. A report sent to the Madrid *corte* on 18 June 1617 by

Juan García de Navia, governor of Santiago de Cuba, acknowledges the existence of thirty-seven refineries in the eastern jurisdiction of the island; their product was by then being exported to northern South America and Spain. However, the very unreliable census taken in 1620 by Bishop Henríquez Almendares de Toledo places the percentage of blacks at only 6.6.[12]

Although the economic development of the island was very slow in the seventeenth century, due to wars, piracy, trade restrictions, and lack of a market for manufactured goods, it was in that period that Cuba consolidated what was to become its "fundamental wealth." The cultivation of cane and the production of sugar, which had begun close to the villages, spread out gradually as the number of slaves grew. Ramiro Guerra could say in discussing that period that "sugar and slaves were practically synonymous terms." [13] This is confirmed in the census taken in 1622, which showed that almost 50 percent of the 30,000 inhabitants of Cuba were black.

In the second half of the eighteenth century, the first coffee groves combined with the growing sugar industry to exploit black labor, and the rapid economic growth of the period is reflected in the importation of large numbers of African slaves. One trader, the marqués of Casa-Enrile, brought more than 14,000 slaves in six years through the port of Havana, and a steadily growing number entered at other points on the island. The marqués, to increase his profits, brought about the repeal of the ordinances of Cáceres that had prohibited the resale of African slaves at a higher price. Consequently, every manual or mechanical skill acquired by a slave represented a rise in his economic value, leaving the door wide open for speculation. Slaves passed from hand to hand like any other merchandise, and their personal condition worsened; they had become objects of exchange. This fact is of great importance in the history of Cuban slavery; because of it the country took on characteristics similar "to the other plantation colonies of the turn of the century." [14]

By 1763 it was calculated that more than 60,000 Africans had entered Cuba.[15] The census taken between 1774 and 1775 at the initiative of the "enlightened" governor, Felipe de Fonsdeviela, marqués de la Torre, which is the first reliable study of the Cuban population, authenticates the presence of the black in the population of the island. This important statistical work tallied a total of 172,620 persons of whom 96,440 (56.4 percent) were white, and 76,180 (43.6

percent) were black. Of the black population, 31,847 were free and 44,333 were slaves. Except for New England and Canada, Cuba had the lowest proportion of slaves of any European colony, 25 percent of its total population. It was the only Antillean island other than Puerto Rico having a majority of white inhabitants.[16]

The census taken in 1719 showed that the population had not changed very much. Whites constituted 56.4 percent, free blacks 19.84 percent, and slaves 23.72 percent.[17] The growth in the number of free people among the black population is greater than that of the slave population in the same period, which demonstrates the relative ease of manumission. According to Alberto Arredondo the percentage of blacks was 43.8 in 1774 and 43.6 in 1796;[18] the black population had diminished slightly. Between 1774 and 1791, the increase in the number of liberated and freeborn blacks, was greater each year than the rise in the number of slaves. But the free introduction of Africans authorized in 1789 and the rapid development of the sugar and coffee industries were to alter that picture radically. Cuba was to become in fact a plantation colony.

Around 1790, the importation of black slaves was of the greatest importance to the Cuban planters. Under the authority of an order issued in 1789, about 20,000 Africans entered the country; but what the planters wanted then was the continuation of freedom in the slave trade. On 24 November 1791, the envoy from the district of Havana obtained a six-year extension of the disposition of 1789, which was later extended indefinitely. An aid to the growth of this free trade was, paradoxically, the slave uprising in Haiti and the consequent rise in the world market of the price of tropical products, especially sugar and coffee. When Cuba replaced Haiti in supplying these products, more than 30,000 immigrants entered the country, settling particularly in the eastern part. Many coffee plantations were established, with a consequent rise in slave labor. By the end of the eighteenth century, the number of slaves had grown dramatically, and the ethnic composition of the country was considerably altered. The German scholar Alexander von Humboldt, during his visit to Cuba (1800–1804), calculated that the total black population was as high as 54 percent, of which 18 percent were free and 36 percent were slaves.[19]

Traditionally, efforts have been made to understate the level of cruelty of Cuban slavery, as well as to claim that the blacks passively accepted an unjust system of exploitation that denied them the status of human beings. But there were attempts to revolt on the part of the slaves who, as we have seen, were becoming very numerous. The rebellion in Puerto Príncipe (today Camagüey) on 11 June 1798 was particularly significant. In the sugar mill of Don Manuel Narciso de Agramonte the slaves, most of them from the African tribe Carabalís, set fire to the plant and killed the overseers of the work squadrons.[20] These attempts at revenge are explained in part by the considerable cruelty that characterized Cuban slavery during this period. The life of a slave in the refinery was harder and more wretched than ever. These sugar mills were no longer little "caldrons"; they were becoming large industrial complexes in which the slave was required to produce the maximum in the minimum time in order to lower production costs. Moreover, the free slave trade made it possible for the *hacendado* to look upon his slave not as a valuable asset, difficult to replace, but as a "product" that could easily be obtained in the marketplace in exchange for sugar, molasses, or rum.

There was profound consternation when news reached the island of the motion made by Miguel Guridi y Alcocer, deputy for Mexico to the 1811 Cortes of Cádiz, proposing abolition of the slave trade, already agreed to by England in 1808. Curiously, many whites—partisans of the suppression of the slave trade and of slavery, as well as some clergy—took it upon themselves to pass the news among the Cuban blacks. When the cortes laid the matter aside, the slaves realized that their liberty could be obtained only through rebellion. During that period, "the black population was highly unified by racial solidarity and collective resentments against the white man's stocks, chains, and whip, and against his laws and customs, which subjected the free Negro to an inferior economic, juridical, and social position, and to constant persecution." [21] This explains why the conspiracy directed by José Antonio Aponte, a free black, spread so rapidly among the slave population of the island. In 1813, the cortes again discussed the problem of abolition—this time secretly—but nothing came of it.

According to Angel Rosenblat, by 1811 the population of Cuba had reached 600,000, of whom 326,000 were blacks, among them 212,000 slaves.[22] The census of 1817, ordered by the intendant, Don Alejandro Ramírez, showed that the population had grown by 132 percent since 1791, and its ethnic composition had changed noticeably. The number of whites stood at 291,021, or 45.96 percent of the total, showing a loss of 10.42 percent; the number of free blacks was 115,691 or 18.32

percent, showing a proportionate loss of 1.52 percent. The slave population, however, had risen to 224,268, or 35.55 percent, with a rise in its proportion of 11.83 percent. According to the statistics presented by Arredondo, there was a marked rise in the number of blacks: from 43.6 percent in 1792 to 55 percent in 1817.[23]

Since 1808 England had prohibited the slave traffic in its dominions, and the Congress of Vienna of 1814 had tried to obtain universal suppression of it. Spain's colonies put pressure on Ferdinand VII, who instructed his plenipotentiaries to oppose the English efforts. The Congress approved only "a general declaration of principles against the traffic" and postponed discussion of this matter to a later time.[24] But the Cubans knew the Spanish monarch would not be able to resist the pressure of the English for long. It was better to give in in a limited way, and this was done in a motion presented to the king on 25 August 1816 by Francisco de Arango y Parreño. A compromise formula, it established the immediate prohibition of the slave trade from those coasts of Africa lying to the north of the equator; for those lying south of that line, the prohibition would date from 22 April 1821. On 23 September 1817 the treaty with England was signed, giving the British warships the right to register the slave ships and creating a mixed arbitration commission with its seat in Havana to resolve problems related to the slave trade.

The threat of abolition of the slave trade and the possible prohibition of slavery was a crisis the colonial *hacendados* tried to overcome by means of the technological aid afforded by the Industrial Revolution, and in 1819, the first complete *zafra*—harvesting and refining of a sugar crop—was achieved with steam machinery in Pedro Diago's refinery, La Fermina. Nevertheless, the census of 1825–27 revealed that the number of slaves, 286,942, was higher than ever, as was the proportion of slaves to the total population. The absolute percentage of blacks totaled 56. This growth in black slave population was due to the continuation of the slave traffic, practiced on a large scale in spite of the treaty of 1817. It is calculated that from 1821 to 1831 no fewer than 60,000 slaves entered Cuba, brought by about 300 slaving expeditions, of which the British cruisers succeeded in capturing less than 4 percent.[25] In *Cecilia Valdés* by Cirilo Villaverde we find an excellent picture of this illegal traffic and also of the subterfuges used to flout international law when a slave ship was captured.

The treaty of 1817 created a new class: the emancipated blacks.

As mentioned above, a tribunal was set up in Havana to rule on any infractions of the treaty. Every time an English ship captured a slave ship, this tribunal had to decide whether previously enslaved blacks were being moved from one place to another in the Spanish dominions or whether new "goods" were being brought from Africa. In the latter case, the Africans were given a purely nominal liberty, being placed for four years under the guardianship of a person who was to teach them to live in a new and completely strange society. These emancipated blacks received worse treatment than the slaves because their guardians had no interest in caring for "something" that was not theirs, at least from a legal point of view. During this period, José Antonio Saco calculated that the annual importation of African blacks was as high as 10,000 and that by 1830 a total of almost 500,000 Africans had entered Cuba.[26]

Slave labor was the basis of the economic peak and the material prosperity that Cuba enjoyed in the first four decades of the nineteenth century. For example, the sugar industry registered a growth in production of 28 percent, explained by the increment in slave population. In 1827 the number of slaves had risen to 286,942, in 1838 to 436,495. If in 1817, when the treaty suppressing the slave traffic was signed, the number of slaves was 199,145 and if we take into consideration that a slave lived an average of fifteen years as an adult, then the only possible explanation for this growth is that the majority of the slaves in Cuba in the period 1830–40 had been brought in fraudulently.[27] Ramiro Guerra wrote: "the entire economic organization of the island in 1833, all the wealth of Cuba, the foundations of society and what could be called the civilization of the period, were based on slavery, and on an illegitimate slavery, with respect to Spanish law and international treaties." [28] From this traffic in human beings, all the colonial authorities received benefits, from the captain-general of the island down to the least municipal functionary. The Spanish merchants established in Havana invested large sums to finance the slaving expeditions and made fat profits (Villaverde has left us a portrait of this type in Don Cándido de Gamboa); and even Queen María Christina received an "ounce of gold" for "each 'sack of charcoal' that had entered Cuba." [29] It was the golden age of slave society and of the most opulent European colony of the period.

The human and social situation of the blacks within this system was frightful. Those born in Africa were called "tribal Negroes," and those born on the island were called "creole Negroes." If they spoke Spanish badly, they were called *bozales* or *bozalones;* if they had an acceptable command of the language of the whites, they were called *ladinos.* Don Fernando Ortiz cites the testimony of an English abolitionist, Wilburforce, who tells about the first moments in the enslavement of the African: slavers would attack a quiet village during the night and, if necessary, burn it.[30] As the inhabitants fled from the fires, they were captured and carried in caravans from the interior of the African continent to the coast, where they were sold to slave traders. They crossed the Atlantic immobilized in the crowded holds of the ships. Many succumbed during the crossing, either during ill-fated insurrections, from illnesses, or just to "lighten the load" in the face of pursuit by a British vessel.

Until 1820, while the trade was permitted, the slaves disembarked on the dock in Havana; after that date, disembarkations took place on beaches or at anchoring grounds, such as the one José Martí saw as a child and to which he gave literary expression in his *Versos sencillos.* From innumerable points on the extensive Cuban coast, the unhappy Africans were taken to the villages where they were sold like remnants from a factory that was being liquidated. Upon receiving Christian names, they were branded on the left shoulder with the surname of the owner. The slave might be destined for domestic service or for work on the coffee plantations or in the sugar refinery, which was considered "Negro prison." There was no comparison between the work of the urban slave and that of the rural one. On this point Humboldt says that "the threats made in an attempt to correct the recalcitrant Negro help us to understand the levels of human deprivation in slavery. The driver of a calash was threatened with the coffee plantation; the coffee worker with the sugar refinery." [31] The punishment imposed on Francisco, in the novel of the same name by Anselmo Suárez y Romero, is an example of this policy.

Abolitionist sentiment began to show itself in the third decade of the nineteenth century. Francisco Arango y Parreño, who had been a decided defender of the slave traffic, sent reports to the king in 1828 and 1832 on the need to suppress the trade. Before that, in 1826, the bishop of Havana, Juan José Díaz de Espada y Landa, in a pastoral letter directed to his parishoners stated that "since the trading of Negroes was prohibited, they were wrong to continue it, and they would in effect be committing a theft if they acquired one."[32] But the champion of the opposition to the illicit slave trade was José Antonio Saco (1797–1879), whose life was a constant effort to obtain political reforms for Cuba and a constant struggle to achieve the suppression of the slave trade and the institution of slavery. His campaign against illicit trading began in 1830 in the *Memoria sobre la vagancia de la isla* [Memorandum on the vagrancy of the island] and was crowned with the publication of the *Historia de la esclavitud* (1875). In the strictly literary field, the first abolitionist novels were being written.

However, public opinion on the island was far removed from the antislavery ideas of this group of young intellectuals. The colonial hacendados could not understand the essential point of Saco's thought: slavery was antiquated because it was uneconomical—slave labor was more costly than wage labor—and, in addition, it caused grave damage to the social fabric of the nation. The sugar refiners still held to the old theory that slave labor was necessary to maintain the stability of the national economy. Thus, in 1838, approval by the British Parliament of the immediate abolition of slavery in all the British dominions produced a commotion in Cuba. It was thought, and rightly, that England would try hard to persuade other countries to prohibit the slave trade and even the practice of slavery.[33]

In November of 1840, David Turnbull arrived in Havana as the British consul and England's commissioner on the Arbitration Tribunal. This radical abolitionist was charged with putting into practice the militant antislave policies of Lord Palmerston. Some of his activities were related to the illegal importation of slaves; others were directed toward clarifying the situation of the "emancipated" slaves and of those who had a right to freedom. But in 1842, with the change of government in England, Turnbull was removed from his post. Because his passionate antislavery sentiments were frustrated and his personal feelings were severely damaged, he determined to work on his own in order to "vindicate himself fully."[34] He conceived a plan to put an end to Spanish domination of the island and to achieve the abolition of slavery by means of an insurrection of free blacks and slaves. The object was to create a republic such as Haiti's with strong ties of dependency to Great Britain. The uprising, prepared for 25 December 1843, was accidentally discovered, and during the very cruel investigatory proceedings that followed—the Conspiración de la Escalera (the Ladder Plot)[35]—the mulatto poet Gabriel de la Concepción Valdés ("Plácido") lost his life and the black writer Juan F. Manzano, filled with terror, grew forever silent. It has been estimated that more than 4,000 people were involved in this plot, and some 400 lost their lives.[36]

In spite of the constant danger of slave rebellions, the white, pro-slave society continued to bring in "bags of charcoal," the name used to designate the Africans.[37] Francisco Coello calculated that there were 436,495 slaves in Cuba in 1841, but in 1846 the number had diminished to 323,759. According to Arredondo, the percentage of blacks in Cuba in 1841 was 58.5—the highest figure thus far—while by 1861 the percentages had been reduced to 43.2.[38]

This decline in the percentage of blacks is explained by the Law of Repression of the Trade, signed in 1845 by Spain. From that time on, the clandestine trade continued, but at a lower and lower rate, until 1872, when the last slave ships arrived in Cuba. The Anglo-American cooperation in the pursuit of slave ships, the crisis in the coffee industry, the mechanization of the cultivation and harvesting of sugar, and the importation of Yucatán Indians and Asiatic settlers were other factors contributing to this decline. From 1845 on, the proportionate growth of the two races was in inverse terms.[39] By the middle of the nineteenth century, "the African slave trade with all its abominable horrors, was a repugnant anachronism, condemned and repudiated by the moral conscience of all civilized nations." [40]

This abolitionist sentiment took on new life with the founding in 1865 of the first Cuban antislavery organization, the Asociación contra la Trata (the Organization against the Slave Trade). Although short-lived—the Overseas Ministry in Madrid never gave it definitive approval—it reflected a state of mind ever more favorable to the disappearance of the "domestic institution," a euphemism for slavery in Cuba. On the other hand, the rich colonial proprietors had had to give up the idea of annexation by the Confederate states as a means of holding on to their "property" indefinitely, because the North had triumphed in the American Civil War. Only two paths were left open to overcome Cuba's political, social, and economic problems: autonomist liberalism or separatism. The plan presented by the Cuban commissioners to the Junta de Información in Madrid (1868) was the one upheld by the liberals: gradual emancipation with indemnity for the slaveholders.[41]

The failure of this commission, because the Spanish government refused to accept the measures recommended by its members, was one of the immediate causes of the first war for Cuban independence on 10 October 1868. Carlos Manuel de Céspedes, initiator of the insurrection in Oriente province, freed his slaves the same day he started the war, and on 27 December 1868 he issued the decree abolishing slavery in Cuba and conceding to the blacks the same rights and duties the white citizens held. In the province of Camagüey, slavery was prohibited on 26 February 1869 by agreement of its Assembly of Representatives. The Cuban constitution of 1869, drawn up by the National Assembly in the city of Guaímaro, enunciated the principle of equality of all citizens without distinction of race or creed.[42]

The war was to last ten years, at the end of which time the Cubans had to negotiate a peace agreement (1878). The capitulation signed on 10 February 1878 recognized in article 3 the right to liberty of all the "slaves who had been in the ranks of the revolutionaries." The irony of conceding freedom to the insurrectionist slaves and keeping enslaved those who had been loyal to the Spanish domination was in fact the death blow to the system. Earlier, in 1870, a new law (la ley de vientres libres) had been imposed, which provided that the offspring of slaves would be manumitted at birth; in 1880 the abolition of salvery was promulgated, with a period of "oversight," which, although recognizing the legal freedom of the slave required him to live under a regimen of protection while he awaited complete freedom. When in 1886 the autonomist party of Cuba succeeded in the total abolition of slavery without indemnity, it was in fact practically extinct. The abolition of slavery can be considered the most "brilliant and glorious conquest and the most beneficial result produced for Cuba by the Ten Years' War."[43]

Once assimilated into the Cuban population, the blacks had taken part in the political process, either on the side of the autonomists, such as Martín Morúa Delgado, or with the separatists, such as Juan Gualberto Gómez, who was one of Martí's closest collaborators. The blacks' political rights were recognized in the constitution of 1901 and reaffirmed in that of 1940. That year the census showed 12.6 percent blacks and 15 percent mulattoes.[44] But in Cuba there has also been a psychological "mulattization." As Fernando Ortiz points out, "Cuban society developed psychologically an imperceptible gradation from white to Negro; a complete fusion occurred, both physiologically and psychologically."[45]

Chapter Two

The Black Theme in Cuban
Literature: A Summary

From their beginnings, Cuban letters constantly reflect the black segment of the population of the island; however, we still do not have available a complete or comprehensive study of the presence of a pattern of black themes in Cuban literature. The work of the ill-fated scholar José Antonio Fernández de Castro cannot be compared with works such as those of Raymond S. Sayers and Gregory Rabassa.[1] The little book by Fernández de Castro was written during his exile in Mexico, without benefit of references or of basic texts; besides suffering from lamentable omissions, especially in the parts concerning the nineteenth-century novel and the vernacular theater, it lacks the systematization and the critical apparatus indispensable to such a study. As for G. R. Coulthard's book, it examines only the abolitionist narrative and the black movement in contemporary poetry, without attempting to show the continuity in the development of the black theme in Cuban literature. And in some cases Coulthard's data are incorrect or uncertain.[2]

I Sixteenth to Eighteenth Century: The Epic, Folklore, and Satire

Treatment of the black theme in Cuban letters dates back to the beginnings of Cuban literary expression. Even in the period before 1790, considered by many to be practically a literary void,[3] we encounter the black theme and the black or mulatto writer. In Silvestre de Balboa's *Espejo de paciencia* (1608), the first poem of known authorship written in Cuba, the black character appears clearly delineated; an "Ethiopian" (rhetorical euphemism for African) is cast as hero and in single combat he vanquishes the French pirate Gilberto Girón.

> Active on our side
> There moved an Ethiopian worthy of praise
> Named Salvador, a courageous Negro,
> One of the toilers of Yara;
> Son of Golomón, a wise old man:
> This man, armed with a machete and a lance,
> When he saw Gilberto approach resolutely,
> Attacked him like a furious lion.
>
> Don Gilberto, when he saw the Ethiopian,
> Immediately prepared for battle:
> And they met; but after the encounter
> The Negro was naked, the Frenchman in armor.
> O thou divine muse, Calliope,
> And thou lovely nymph, Aglaia, grant
> That my pen describe
> The valor and gallantry of this Negro.
>
> O Salvador, the creole, upright Negro,
> May your fame spread and never wane:
> For in praise of such a good soldier
> It is well that neither tongue nor pen tire.
> And because I offer you this honor,
> Let no malevolent person suspect
> That I write this showing affection
> Toward a Negro, captured and enslaved without cause.[4]

As is evident from the verses cited, this "Salvador, the memorable Negro," the first black protagonist of Cuban literature, is a rhetorical hero of the Renaissance epic, as is his father, Golomón, the "wise old man." The plight of the black has become literature, but an exterior vision of the character directs the creation of the image—a colonial Negro, upright and courageous, but without force or special flavor. This vision is such that Balboa cannot identify with the slave; he is acted upon by a social prejudice that is very clear in the last lines. Thus, Salvador, a Bayamese slave, is transformed into a stereotype that obliterates his authentic human value.

The African brought with him his magical-mystical world and his folklore, both of which made their mark on the psychological and cultural makeup of the Cuban people. As Ramón Guirao has pointed out, there is a "formidable, uninterrupted tradition which begins with the so-called 'poeta gallo' (rooster poet) or 'gourd poet' (because the gourd was used as an accompanying instrument of the African tribal meetings on the island)—a tradition carried out in the funeral chants of the liturgy, the slumber songs, masquerade songs, drum songs, fiesta tunes, guarachas, and invocations and in farces written in Africanoid jargon, décimas, and carols." [5] One of the most interesting of these manifestations is the "snake-killing dance," performed at the typically Afro-Cuban Three Kings Day Fiesta.[6] There is extant a text of this dance, which dates, in all probability from the eighteenth century:

> Mommy, mommy!
> Yen, yen, yen.
> The snake is biting me!
> Yen, yen, yen.
> The snake is eating me!
> Yen, yen, yen.
> The snake is swall'wing me!
> Yen, yen, yen.[7]

The rhythm and spirit that pervade this poem are characteristic of the mulatto poetry of the twentieth century.

Don Antonio López Prieto, in the introduction of his Parnaso Cubano, has saved from oblivion some very mediocre décimas by the mulatto poet Juana Pastor.[8] We have very little information about this writer, other than that she was born in Havana, that she was a teacher, and that she lived and wrote around the end of the eighteenth century. She knew Latin and taught the most distinguished ladies of the Cuban capital. In the poems that López Prieto salvaged we cannot discern any African inflection; although the poet is deeply influenced by the culture of this period, she reveals herself in these lines as a powerful, feminine, and sensual personality, very favorably disposed to male company.

Carlos M. Trelles in his *Bibliografía cubana de los siglos XVII y XVIII* cites a curious epigrammatic décima written around 1789 by Manuel González de Sotolongo.[9] This little composition, the only one we have by this author, is written in macaronic Latin, and in it the theme of racial prejudice appears clearly for the first time as far as we know. It is a barbed criticism directed at Manuel del Socorro Rodríguez (1758–1818) and his "Aeotiopiae qualitatis." According to this vulgar and malevolent poem, Rodríguez, a Cuban emigrant to New Granada, a librarian in Santa Fè de Bogotá, and the founder of the *Papel periódico* (1791) of that city, was a mulatto. He had been born in Bayamo, of poor parents, and had devoted himself to manual tasks since childhood. In spite of his humble origins, he had managed to acquire an extraordinary erudition, which served to bring him the position of librarian in the capital of New Granada.

II *The Nineteenth Century: Poetry, Drama, and the Novel*

It has been seen that the greatest period of Cuba's economic development began in the last decade of the eighteenth century. As would be expected, the use of the black theme in literature grew more frequent in proportion to the growth of the African slave trade. We must not forget that during this time the indexes of population showed the largest percentages of blacks in the demographic evolution of Cuba, and the poetry of the time reflects Cuba's transformation into a "plantation colony." J. M. Heredia (1803–37) is obviously referring to the injustice of the trade and the fundamental immorality of the institution of slavery in this very well-known verse from his "Himno del desterrado" (1825) when he asks:

if the clamor of the insolent tyrant,
and the doleful groans of the slave,
and the cracking of the horrifying whip
are all that is heard in your fields?

A black poet Juan Francisco Manzano (1797–1859) was a slave, and if indeed it is true that, "by a design of history," he was obliged "to ignore the voice of his race and silence his plans for an aesthetic revolt,"[10] he left us the authentic testimony of his touching experience in a document invaluable for an inside understanding of the period, the *Apuntes autobiográficos* (1839). In addition, in the sonnet "Mis treinta años" he synthesizes that experience in a moving way:

> It is thirty years since I first saw this land;
> For thirty years that sad misfortune has
> Assaulted me from every side, as I cried out;
> But for me, war, which I bore
> With vain sighs, is nothing,
> If I compare it, O God, with what I lack.[11]

A very different case is that of Gabriel de la Concepción Valdés (1809–44), better known by the pseudonym Plácido. Ignorance and romantic idealism made of this unfortunate mulatto poet the incarnation of the noble savage and the "newly coined" hero—the natural poetic genius freely expressing himself. Plácido was neither of these. Son of a quadroon and a white ballerina, the color of his skin was practically that of the privileged race. Because he had stayed in the Royal House of Charity, where he began his education, he could have passed for a white. An extemporizer of popular verse and a versifier of the impossible, he has nevertheless left us a few fine poems that save his name from oblivion. Implicated without grounds in the so-called Ladder Conspiracy, he was condemned to death, and in order to save his own life, denounced the purest Cubans of his day, Domingo del Monte and José de la Luz y Caballero.[12] In his work as a whole, it is difficult to discover the black point of view; only in an "Epigrama satírico" can we discern a preoccupation with race:

> If you tell everyone, Arcino,
> That those who have something of Guinea in
> Their skin and noses are of low breeding
>
> Then, Arcino, you must confess
> That it is a proven folly
> If your roof is of glass
> To throw stones at your neighbor.[13]

Although born in Venezuela, Domingo del Monte (1804–53) was a Cuban by choice and destiny. His famous literary gatherings in Matanzas and Havana became in fact an adequate substitute for the unsuccessful attempt to form an Academy of Cuban Letters. Del Monte, an authentic humanist, was the catalyzing agent for the first generation of Cuban romantics. Literary life on the island from 1830 to 1840 cannot be fully understood without an awareness of his guiding influence, although he generally published very little. Dramas such as *El conde Alarcos* by José Jacinto Milanés are products of these gatherings, as are such novels as *Francisco,* the passionate anti-slavery work by Anselmo Suárez y Romero. "An upright spirit, [del Monte] always showed an abolitionist point of view toward slavery," [14] and he brought these ideas to his poetry. In the fourth of his *Romances cubanos* (1833), entitled "La patria," he puts into the mouth of a beater his ideas about the Cuban "domestic institution":

I could never hear
Without anger boiling in my soul
The barbarous, atrocious crack of
The whip on human flesh.

Only the sweat of my brow,
Free, upright, and honorable,
Watered the sown furrow
With its sacred drops . . .

And I prefer living proud,
Poor, but free from stain
To living in an infamous opulence,
Bought at an infamous price.[15]

One of the first generation of romantics, José Jacinto Milanés (1814–63) wrote poems in which the black or the mulatto is in the foreground. In the legend "El negro alzado" (1835), we encounter a strong narration of the misfortunes and punishments of the slave, from his childhood until he finds it necessary to rebel and run away; in "El poeta envilecido" (1837), referring to Plácido, he clearly touches the theme of racial discrimination:

And if fate made him [the poet]
black or bronze,
    unfortunate, he!
for his horizon is gloomy,
his air dry, his sun cold,
his love bitter! [16]

Francisco Muñoz del Monte (1800–63) adopts an opposite attitude. His poem "La mulata," published in Havana in 1845, is erotic,
full of color and musicality, and is clearly an antecedent of the
sensualist treatment of the black theme, where the mulatto woman
becomes the incarnation of the most primitive sexual desires. The
sexual vision of this new bronze Venus is also found in a composition by Bartolomé Crespo Borbón (1811–71), an author of
sainetes and farces who had become famous under the pseudonym
Creto Gangá. In the text that concerns us here, he does not attempt
the grotesque Afro-Spanish jargon with which he had caricatured
the language of the bozales in the plays that had given him such
acclaim; he uses instead a limpid Spanish from which emerges,
with a stylized and sensual tone, the opulent figure of the graceful
mulatto woman.

dove with tail outstretched,
who happily struts about;
like a chocolate mill
gracefully manipulated.

In the opinion of Emilio Ballagas, only Diego Vicente Tejera (1844–
1903) and José Martí (1853–95), "of their century, make a strong
impression in Negro verse." [17] Tejera, the poet of tropical sensuality
who had sung the delights of "La Hamaca," cultivated the black
theme, with clear social implications, in two poems, "Negro y
blanco" (1876) and "Colores" (1878). The first is the dramatic con-
traposition of relations between the two races, at the childhood and
the adult levels:

The child who laughs is white . . .
The one who caresses him is black.

The executioner is white;
The man who is his victim, black.

The same ingenuity of expression and the melodramatic touch are felt in "Colores," although here the relationship is between the "señorita" and her poor slave: "How white would be the black woman! / How black the white!" if "the colors of the face showed in their facial expressions."

In an impeccable sonnet to "The Death of the Slave," Mercedes Matamoros (1858–1906) sang with the impassive and refined elegance of the Parnassians. Therefore, we do not feel in this poem the deep, human pain of the slave beaten down in his rebellion. The poet contemplates the dying slave with the objective coolness of a pseudo-classical statue, which gives her composition the hard touch of something that has been achieved with a contemplative, aesthetic cerebralism:

> He still hears in the distance the howling
> Of the mastiff, sniffing in the field,
> And the sharp crack of the whip, even in
> The arms of hard death.[18]

In contrast, in the poem "1868" (1892), Enrique Hernández Miyares (1859–1914) sees the black as a kind of allegorical figure of liberty: the *mambí* who has been a slave and commits suicide rather than fall into slavery again.

In José Martí, too, we find an identification with the black and his libertarian ideal. In Martí's work the theme of racial integration constantly recurs, as can be seen in his speech "El plato de lentejas," in his essay "Mi raza," [19] or in the fine children's story "La muñeca negra," published in *La edad de oro* in October 1889. As in Hernández Miyares, "the antislavery theme in Martí runs in anti-Spanish channels";[20] a proof of this is one of the poems in his *Versos sencillos* (1891). Here the traumatic childhood experience of witnessing the unloading of a slave ship is turned into an expression of the black so totally lacking in colorism—in negritude—that, in the tempestuous light of this poem, he is elevated to the level of a universal and suffering human being. Martí destroys the distance between the writer-subject and the black-object, and when this integration is achieved, the poet understands that he, too, is in servitude.

The lightning cuts a furrow in the gloomy, threatening cloud:
The ship spews the Negroes by the hundreds through the big
    door.

The fierce wind broke the thick-topped mastic trees:
The line moved, the line of naked slaves.

A different, softer tone than that shown by Martí in this violent
eau-forte (a water-color technique) on the slave trade is felt in the
poem by Manuel Serafín Pichardo (1865–1937), "El último esclavo,"
where the black is reduced to an "idiotized" being, a sort of infrahuman creature who does not understand the violent experiences
that have marked his life. Although the "domestic institution" is
described for us in its harshest aspects, this poor black man finds
himself so degraded psychologically and morally that he looks back
with nostalgia to his days of slavery. His eyes, "blued with age," are
fixed on his "former pleasure,"

his drum and his vegetables,
his patch of ground and his machete,
the horseshoe shape of the stocks,
and the ironwork of the shackles.

Pichardo gives literary form to the old topic of Cuban slave society:
the happy slave, happy because he is incapable of perceiving how
terribly inhuman his situation is.

Nineteenth-century Cuban poetry in the popular vein shows innumerable examples of the treatment of the black. Ballagas, in the
anthology cited above, speaks of the existence of masquerade songs,
satires, cries, work songs from the sugar mills, and "a rebellion song,
that we hear from the lips of an African slave woman, Ma Chambá." [21]
But perhaps the most interesting of the traditional poetry is that
which shows crossbreeding—poetry that we can classify uncon-
ditionally as mulatto or mestizo. Examples of this poetry would be
the guarachas, sones, and other songs and dances of the island.
Roberto Fernández Retamar, in La poesía contemporánea en Cuba
(1927–1953), cites two examples of the guarachas, "undoubtedly
coming before Guillén and Ballagas":

Saintly mulatto woman,
Put a robe on,
And come to the window
To hear my serenade.
Goodbye, child!
What a pretty foot!
With hard-toed shoe
Mulatto woman, I'll buy you.[22]

Emilio Ballagas also refers to the existence of love songs in Africanoid jargon,[23] such as the following one found in our own family tradition:

Your eyes am sweeter dan de quanabaná,*
Tastier and fresher dan de chirimoyá,
And you laugh whiter dan de white lily,
And you lips de same pink as de mamey.

I gon' die if you ain't my sweetheart.
By de Holy God, black girl, don' kill me.
And don' lemme die o' sadness, little black girl:
Gimme a little kiss with you little pink mouth.

And dose eyes dat'll never have catarats
And dat light up jes' like a little glowworm
Sure muss have a little waist
Dat moves and wriggles like a snake.

Finally, we must mention the work of Francisco Calcagno (1827–1903), *Poetas de color.* Edited in Havana in 1878, Calcagno's anthology is a defense and a vindication of the intellectual and artistic capacity of the blacks. It is, after all, an antislavery work, because it exalts the poetic virtues of these black writers while it cites cultural reasons for comparing them equally with whites. Except for Plácido and Manzano, the versifiers studied by Calcagno in this tract lack real importance in Cuban literature. They include Juan Estrada, Vicente Silveira, and José Carmen Díaz. It was, incidentally, this edition of 1878 that served to buy Díaz's manumission.

---

* Accents are misplaced on final syllable of line for rhythmic effect.

The Afro-Cuban jargon, poorly rendered in the translation cited above and a caricature of the Spanish spoken by the blacks of the island, became one of the most important comic devices of the Cuban so-called *teatro bufo* of the nineteenth and twentieth centuries. As José Juan Arrom has pointed out, the creator of this genre, which in Cuba is known as *criollo*—typical or "vernacular" theater—was Francisco Covarrubias (1775–1850), who adapted the *sainetes* of the Madrid author Ramón de la Cruz to the current Cuban fashion and milieu.[24] No composition by Covarrubias is extant, but there are some by his immediate followers, who exploited all the scenic possibilities of the different types of black people. Thus, still alive in these farces is the graceful black woman, the little black "professor," the native African, and the picturesque, tawdry fellow from the mangrove grove, a curious mixture of Andalusian and African folkways.

Bartolomé Crespo Borbón, "Creto Gangá" (1811–71), decided to paint "negros de nación" (slaves born in Africa, who mumbled Spanish badly). *La boda de Pancha Jutía y Canuto Raspadura* (1847) "is a picture without a plot, brimming with characters, . . . which defies any attempt at organization."[25] In this little piece, colonial blacks and mulattoes as well as natives of Africa are depicted. Caricature of the language spoken by the blacks is always the primary source of comedy.

The same thing happens in the so-called *obras catedráticas* ("professorial" works).[26] The blacks' dialectal forms are still an object of jest, as are their customs and their mimicry of the white man, but now a more grotesque element is added. These "Negro professors," confused by a pedantic erudition, express themselves in a resounding and florid language, totally inconsistent and sprinkled at intervals with a deformed phonetism, in order to establish a comic effect. Both the actors who produced these works and the authors who dashed them off were white. In this vein, we have the *sainetes* of Francisco Fernández, *Los negros catedráticos* (1868) and *El bautizo* (1868); and from this same writer in collaboration with Pedro N. Pequeño, *El negro cheche* (1868). As an example of this tendency, consider the words of Crispín, the "Negro professor," in the first scene of the play of the same title: "There's no similicutance possible when one is dealing with people of precise education, who rise by their own efforts above the equinuptial."[27]

Aside from these grotesque caricactures, the black theme is almost completely absent from the theater of that period. One exception is Alfredo Torroella (1845–79), a poet of the second generation of romantics, who wrote a three-act drama in prose, *El mulato* (1870), during his exile in Mexico. This work, which belongs to the strong abolitionist current, presents the conflict of the slave in love with his mistress, a conflict resolved by his suicide. According to Arrom, "in its day it merited very favorable commentaries from the Mexican press, but now its laurels have wilted." [28]

In the novel that takes the blacks and their problems as its central theme, two periods in the nineteenth century stand out with some clarity. The first, which includes those works written between 1835 and 1841, is characterized by an abolitionism with a romantic stamp, in which are present, on the one hand, the liberal and rationalist ideas of the Enlightenment and the French Revolution and, on the other hand, the *costumbrista* and descriptive accents of the human and natural features of Cuba. This *costumbrismo* in some cases achieves notes of authentic realism. Almost all of these narratives were written under the auspices of the *tertulias* of Domingo del Monte and follow the ideas of the men who gathered around this humanist.

Juan Francisco Manzano's *Apuntes autobiográficos* (1839) is a kind of "protonovel"—the raw material (suffering, punishment, and misery of the slave) for the antislavery novel in its content of denunciation and testimony. Félix Tanco y Bosmoniel (1797–1871), in his novelette *Petrona y Rosalía* (1838), initiates another of the themes of this type of story, showing us the second of the fundamental thematic levels— the corruption of the white man through his possession of blacks and his concubinage with the black woman. Whites and blacks unite in a hateful act that satisfies the basest appetites of the master. The mulatto is the product of this forced relationship and if she is female, she finds herself condemned to suffering the same fate as her mother. *Cecilia Valdés* (1839), by Cirilo Villaverde (1812–94), besides being a broad view of the colonial slave society, represents the fusion of both themes with the tragedy of the vicious circle from which it is impossible to escape. These topics, so obvious in the Villaverde's novel, are also developed by Anselmo Suárez y Romero in his *Francisco* (1839).

The opposite view is given to us by Gertrudis Gómez de Avellaneda (1814–73) in *Sab* (1841). This famous Cuban lyrical poet, expatriated and far removed from direct knowledge of slavery, wrote an abolitionist novel that takes up and is the echo of the European romantic illusion. The mulatto is seen as the noble savage, and this caricature is weighted with the lachrymose and sentimental ballast of the period. Avellaneda had a lyrical vision of the black character, not the dramatic one necessary for the circumstances of Cuba at that time.

For some time thereafter, Cuban fiction writers did not dare to touch the black theme, not even in private editions. This fact must be attributed to the savage repression that had occurred in 1844, the "year of the whip," as it is traditionally known on the island. Thus, the second period of the nineteenth-century black novel must be placed between 1875 and the end of the colonial administration. During this second period, the black character is treated with more depth and delineated with greater authenticity. It is the time of realism and naturalism, as seen in the pages of *Romualdo: Uno de tantos* by Francisco Calcagno, a novel written in 1869 but completely unknown until its publication in 1891. A tendency toward the nineteenth-century concept of realism can also be seen in the work of Antonio Zambrana (1842–1922), who reelaborates the old theme of *Francisco* in the novel of the same title (1875), and of Ramón Meza (1861–1911), who in *Carmela* (1886) continues the mulatto line of Villaverde. Finally, with Martín Morúa Delgado (1857–1910), the naturalist school of Emile Zola enters the scene. In fact, Morúa Delgado is the first in Cuba to write novels of this type, applying the "experimental" method to the analysis of the conflicts of the black at the time of the liquidation of the colony. His *Sofía* (1891) is an original version of the problem of the blacks and their environment.

III   The Twentieth Century and the Negroist Mode

Independence had been achieved in 1902, and in the first years of the Republic the black theme was absent from literary works. In the first fifteen years of independence, "this phenomenon of Negro 'absenteeism' exists not only in indigenous Cuban literature but in music and painting as well." [34] This is surprising because it was during this period that ethnographic research was begun by Fernando Ortiz (1881–1970), the eminent Africanist, whose most important contribution to the study of Cuban culture was precisely that of showing the blacks' contribution to the making of Cuban society.

The slavery theme is touched tangentially by Francisco J. Pichardo (1873–1941) in his poem "El trapiche," where the black appears, first, as the "country slave" and then is heard as a distant musical background:

> While, muffled and far away,
> . . . the song of the African Negroes
> . . . disappears in the lazy distance.[29]

Two principal poets of the postmodernist period in Cuba, Regino E. Boti (1878–1959) and José Manual Poveda (1888–1926), were mulattoes, but according to Fernández de Castro, "there is not a trace of his Negro origins in [the works of] the first, and in the second, it is exceptional for the Negro theme to be touched upon."[30] This is incorrect, for Boti, in his "Canción de cuna de la negra esclava," has given us one of the most passionate and moving songs of the Negro soul; and in Poveda we can sense the African accent in two compositions, "Serenata" and especially "El grito abuelo." In this intense poem, the primitive ancestral call of the poet's African background had an extraordinary force of expression. In the incantation of Afro-Cuban music, this cultivated poet felt a sort of "throwback," a regression to the primary and atavistic essences of his mulatto being. The rumba and the comparsa had not yet taken on the characteristic expression of conspicuous onomatopoeic primitivism it was to acquire later, but one can already find in Poveda's composition the violent and tumultous frenzy, the cathartic liberation of elemental passions that were to be an essential note in later poems of this type.

> Song of the shadow, cry of the earth,
> which incites the vertigo of the afterdance,
> repeats, convokes, confuses and appeals,
> surreptitious signal, Oh!, which reaches us,
>
> distant and unknown,
> and from that time it wanders, awes, and hides,

dry, alone, mute, vain, black, broken,
cry of the earth,
somber diatribe,
the only sound
of the faraway pain.

A poem of the same theme as Poveda's, but with a technique that makes it a direct antecedent of what would later be called Afro-Cuban poetry, is "La comparsa" (1916) by Felipe Pichardo Moya (1892–1958). This poem comes close to the tone of a Tallet or a Ballagas, but the purely phonetic possibilities of words as a means of expressing African rhythms have not yet been sensed.

Under the light of the big lanterns
we see the mahogany torsos that shine with sweat.
The hoarse, monotonous music evokes a thousand things.[31]

It is obvious that the fascinations of the blacks' music and dance had been discovered, but nobody had hit upon the poetic expression to capture it faithfully.

Pichardo did not cultivate the black theme only in its coloristic and folkloric aspects; in "El poema de las cañaverales" (1926), this poet, who was always filled with concern for Cuba, senses all the agony of the black on the sugar plantations. In "Filosofía del Bronce," a pathetic view of copulation between the black woman and the white man by force of the whip, the mulatto woman is seen in a new light:

And this is how you came to us,
sister of ours and of the others,
supreme flower of injustice
who make a wild colt
of the fondling dove.

The first example of black poetry—also called Afro-Cuban, mulatto, or "negroitic"[32]—is "Bailadora de rumba" by Ramón Guirao, published in the literary supplement of the Diario de la Marina, 8 April 1928.[33] This type of poetry flourished for a relatively short time, but by 1937 its cycle was already considered to be at an end.[34] Most scholars agree that the work of José Juan Arron is the most serious study attempted of this poetic phenomenon.[35] Black poetry is, of course, not peculiar to Cuba; Luis Palés Matos in Puerto Rico was undoubtedly the initiator of the movement.

We can see the roots of negroism in contemporary Cuban poetry, first, in the negrophilia that struck the European continent beginning with the "nebulous, imprecise origins of cubism," and, second, in the traditional black poetry that existed alongside the *décima* of the rural white man and the cultivated composition of the literate poet.[36] Undoubtedly, the impulse came from France and from the fashion for African things that followed the ethnographic research of Leo Frobenius (1873–1938); this poetic genre was not "a 'graft' or an 'offshoot,' but a return to the large body of folkloric tradition." [37] Thus, we find ourselves witnessing a curious phenomenon in literary relations. The black theme became fashionable when it found aesthetic validation in the work of European artists, and suddenly the *criollo* poets found themselves in the delightful position of having right at home what their European models were seeking abroad—to wit, African folklore and craftwork, jazz, the rumba, and Josephine Baker, all of which are made use of in Cuban poetry. This folklore lived and still lives in the inner soul of the Cuban people, and many of these poetic texts, essentially artistic, have become "lyrics" of songs, for example, some of the *sones* of Nicolás Guillén.

In addition to this fashion for black folklore, we can also find in Afro-Cuban poetry a learned use of the rhetoric of the period. Even the most uncultivated reader can see that black poetry utilizes to the utmost the "imaginative-sensorial wealth hidden in the Spanish phoneme," [38] this technique being characteristic of the "jitanjaphoric" or nonsensical poetry, for example. Thus, Emilio Ballagas writes in his "Comparsa habanera":

> With duster feathers
> from a talking parrot
> the brown Fermina Quintero
> adorns herself.
> With the green plumes
> of the green parrot

This indeed seems like an echo of the Mariano Brull of "Verdehalago":

> Verdancy and greenness
> Greenness and verdure.
> Green, double green
> Of cabbage and lettuce

Two fundamental directions can be noted in Afro-Cuban poetry: one starts with a coloristic, external, and sensual view of the Negro theme and seeks sensorial pleasure from pure sound, from rhythm, and from the erotic, ridiculous, or piquant situation; another seeks a deeper comprehension of the black man, penetrating his inner being either by way of the magical-mystical or through his social problems.[39] Of these, the first was the more developed, and it also aged more rapidly. Examples of this kind of poetic negroism might be "Bailadora de rumba" by Ramón Guirao (1908–49), "La rumba" by José Z. Tallet (1893–), and "Comparsa habanera" by Emilio Ballagas (1908–54). On the other hand, "Liturgia" by Alejo Carpentier (1904–), "Sensemayá" by Nicolás Guillén (1902–), and "Hermano negro" by Regino Pedroso (1896–) are good examples of the second-mentioned tendency. In Pedroso's poem, blacks are seen in their social context, with no concession to "local color." Moreover, the poet addresses the black man and admonishes him to abandon all the "touristic" attributes that have brought him the attention of the white man. In this song to universal brotherhood, the black must quit being Negro in the picturesque sense, in order to assume his authentic human role:

> Negro, brother Negro,
> silence your maracas a little.
>
> Negro, brother Negro,
> muffle your bongo a little.
>
> Are we not more than Negro?
> Are we not more than *jacará* singers?
> Are we not more than rumbas, black lewdness, and minstrels?
> Are we not more than grimace and color,
> grimace and color?

The poet who has expressed "the essential quality of the common black and mulatto tradition in Cuba with the greatest universality and grace of style" is undoubtedly Nicolás Guillén.[40] A mulatto himself, Guillén has a faculty for intuiting the black world, which reveals itself in *Motivos de son* (1930), where he adopts the rhythmic structure of the so-called eastern *son* for his poetic compositions. He was the first who dared to "utilize the language of the Negroes" with a function that was both aesthetic and expressive of the virtues of his race, instead of the comic or caricatural function of the *teatro bufo* of the nineteenth century.[41]

But we should be deceiving ourselves if we thought Guillén did not include in his vision the black's genial aspects. We find in his work a desire to bring these aspects back to their initial purity, to the clear joy of the mulatto, by peeling off the crust that fashion had attached to them. Thus, he undertakes a "return voyage" in search of the *son entero* (the complete *son)*. This stands out clearly in his poem "Guitarra":

> Always high, not fallen,
> bring its smile and its plaint;
> Let it sink into life
> its amianthine claws.

> Take it, guitarist:
> wash the alcohol out of your mouth
> and on that guitar, play
> your whole *son*

> The *son* of mature love,
> your whole *son;*
> the *son* of the open future,
> your whole *son;*
> the *son* of the foot on the wall,
> your whole *son.*

We should also mention the poet's deep understanding of the mythical world of the black ("Sensemayá"), of the most traditional Castilian metric forms ("El abuelo"), and of the most recent finds of avant-garde poetry ("Velorio de Papá Montero").

But Guillén's most substantive contribution is the poetic illumination of the Cuban's mulatto nature and the ethical, aesthetic, and
biological harmonization of the two "motherlands" that gave the
Cuban people their being. In the "Balada de los dos abuelos," he
says,

Shadows that only I see
my two grandfathers go with me.

Both the same size,
black longing and white longing,
both the same size,
they cry out, dream, weep, and sing,
sing . . . sing . . . sing . . .

Blackness then, has ceased to be a theme of color and has returned
to its pristine condition: one seed, with the other, becomes the being
of the poet. Poetry, rather than being black, mulatto, or Cuban, is
simply poetry, a special form of understanding. So, in Guillén, the
black theme ceases to be a fashion; the poet has established its
substance.

In the drama, we encounter the same phenomenon we observed in
the poetry. In the first decades of the twentieth century, the presence
of the black theme is sporadic; it is touched upon very tangentially
in the so-called cultivated theater. The black or the mulatto is a
very secondary character in this drama, almost always reduced to
the level of a domestic servant. She is seen in this role in *Tembladera*
(1916) by José A. Ramos (1885–1946), although we should note with
regard to this play that the lively little mulatto woman is captured
with her most characteristic features, at the same time that she adds,
in the song she sings, the knavish creole flavor that serves as an
introduction to the play.

The opposite occurs in other theatrical pieces. The traditional
Cuban *bufo* genre, "with a flourishing life during this period," [42]
stereotypes definitively the little, slangy, "wise-guy" black man and
"beslippered" black woman, as well as the *gallego* (derogatory term
for the Spanish immigrant). Of this triangle, the black man is perhaps

the principal character.[43] Music is also an essential element, and thus the definitive structure of the plays evolves. These farces on a current subject, nearly always political, were divided into several independent *cuadros*, between which were intercalated musical numbers, the last of which was invariably a conga.

The extemporaneous work of the authors and the improvisations of the actors play a very important role in these plays,[44] where, in contrast to the peninsular dramas, the black is associated with creole liveliness and is a symbol of it. The mulatto woman, for her part, is seen in her most vulgar and erotic aspects. This is, as Arrom has pointed out, the Cuban version of the Italian *commedia dell' arte*.[45]

The renovation in Cuban theater, started around 1927,[46] begins to bear its best fruit far into the fourth decade of this century. In this movement for theatrical improvement, we can see a strong tendency to bring Cuban problems to the stage, and thus to bring in the blacks and their conflictive situation in the heart of Cuban society. In this theater of marked social emphasis, the use of the black or mulatto is constant, as is the theme of the discrimination suffered by the black Cuban.

Marcelo Salinas (1889–) presents in *El mulato* (1940) the old theme of racial prejudices. But here the subject is no longer the slave who overcomes conflict by means of suicide; Daniel Cortés, the mulatto secretary of a senator of the Republic, discovers that his boss has committed fraud and launches into a militant journalism as the only weapon for improving the society into which it has been his lot to be born. The same objectives can be observed in the theater of Paco Alfonso (1906–). In *Hierba hedionda* (1951), the theme of racial discrimination reaches the highest level. A play in three acts, it is in reality a theatrical experiment; moving pictures, lights, dance, music, and song are used to emphasize the adversity of the black. The same techniques are exploited by Alfonso in *Yari-Yari, mamá Olúa* (1941) to denounce the crime of slavery. This play, a text for a musical that has not yet been put to music, relates the tragic vicissitudes of an African tribe on a Cuban plantation up to the point where they decide to commit mass suicide, as the only way to regain their liberty.[47]

The black vision offered by the theater of Flora Díaz Parrado is very different. *Juana Revolico* purports to be an image of blackness achieved by means of the elemental shock of sexual passions with

African liturgy. It turns out to be a *costumbrista* picture of the lowest classes in Santiago de Cuba, with the usual love triangle. Another woman, Teté Casuso, has brought the black theme to her drama, but with a different tone. *Realengo 18* (1939) is a drama in three acts in which the theme of rural evictions is developed. But the black in this play is not just a secondary character: Lino Alvarez, a typical Cuban black, turns out to be the chief of the rural revolutionary movement that fights boldly against the exploitation practiced by the big landholders.

Other contemporary Cuban playwrights have touched on the black theme in their plays, more or less in passing. For example, Juan Domínguez Arbelo (1909–), in *Sombras del solar* (1937), presents the eternal dream of the mulatto woman—to marry a white man; Luis A. Baralt (1892–1969), in *Junto al río* (1938), gives us the figure of Indalecio Ajuria, a black garbage collector "who makes a joyful impression on the public without any need to descend from his status as a man to that of the slangy, farcical nincompoop";[48] and Oscar Valdés Hernández, in *Nuestra gente* (1944), incidentally dramatizes the perennial topic of racial discrimination. The mulatto flavor of all of Cuban society is captured by Relando Ferrer (1925–) in *La hija de Nacho* (1951) and, with admirable theatrical effect, by Carlos Felipe (1914–) in *El chino* (1947).

The curious and significant absence of the black theme from the literature of the first years of the Republic, which we have observed in the poetry and in the theater, is also noticeable in the prose fiction. In the opinion of Fernández de Castro, the lack is more acute in this genre.[49] In fact, until the publication in 1924 of *Mersé* by Félix Soloni (1900–68), it is very difficult to find a novel in which a black is the principal character. Alejo Carpentier has explained this as a product of the attitude of the cosmopolitan writers, who were ashamed of the presence of the black on the island.[50]

El negrero (1933) by Lino Novás Calvo (1905–), a sort of novelistic biography of the fabulous Pedro Blanco, is an attempt to get into step with the new techniques in fiction. This is achieved by means of an objective, bare, and direct vision of the subject; the crime of our forebears is relived, limited to a precise recounting of the facts and devoid of any lyrical or subjective element. On the other hand, in

¡Ecué-Yamba-O! (1933) by Alejo Carpentier (1904–) we are offered the tragedy of the contemporary Cuban black in the framework of the sugar industry. However, this novel is not just the job of a pamphleteer, or a pseudosocial declaration. Carpentier means to capture the essence of blackness and the black environment, beginning with its roots, by placing himself in the magical-mystical world of this black man. In *El reino de este mundo* (1949), using a more straightforward technique, the author shows us, against the background of the slave rebellion in Haiti, the awakening of the black consciousness to a sense of liberty and justice and, as a consequence of this awakening, the rejection of the "kingdom of this world," once it is understood—a rejection that necessarily leads to a resolution to take on tasks for this world's betterment.

We can find this preoccupation with the magical and primitive aspects of the black being also in the contemporary Cuban short story. Although the social problems and the state of material and spiritual desolation in which the black is found are a constant theme in this genre, as we observe in "Cuartillo pa tiñosa" by José M. Carballido Rey (1913–), it seems that the finest successes in this area are found in the attempts to reelaborate African legends brought to Cuba by the slaves. In *Cuentos negros de Cuba* (1940) by Lydia Cabrera (1900–), we have a pure literary version of black mythology, in which, however, the white "translator" managed to include the marks of her own personality. Gerardo del Valle (1898–), on the contrary, prefers to dig around among these legends to discover the causes that determine the behavior of today's mulatto, as is clear in his "Cuentos del Cuarto Fambá" (ca. 1950). Finally, we must not forget that "Viaje a la semilla" by Alejo Carpentier is made possible by the "strange deeds" of that black who seems to have escaped the dictatorship of the clock.

We have come a long way since the good Salvador, a creole, made his entrance into the literature of Cuba, spurred on by the Renaissance. Since then, he has been present in the history of Cuban literature in various disguises and with various attributes, according to the literary fashion of the time. But in this succession of tragic costumes, with picturesque or grotesquely farcical illumination, we have seen a progressive refinement in the literary definition of his person, especially in the novel and in poetry. And this constant progress toward greater authenticity has been possible to the extent that we have ceased to fear a society that has conspired to keep writers from using him as their subject. This is the greatest difficulty the poet, playwright, or novelist has had to face in trying to capture and express the authentic human profile of the black. Let us move on now to a study of the advances and possible retrogressions in the characterization of the black protagonist in the Cuban novel.

Chapter Three

The Early Manifestations of the Abolitionist Narrative

The first purely literary manifestations of the abolitionist idea appeared in authors who belonged to the third clearly defined Cuban generation. The members of this generation, whose birth dates were around 1800, had to oppose the immoralities of the colonial regime; this was the beginning of the atmosphere of tension that was to be the principal characteristic of nineteenth-century Cuban life. This was the generation of the "liberators"—frustrated in Cuba—the twelfth in the generational movements established by José Juan Arrom in his *Esquema generacional de las letras hispanoamericanas*.[1] The conflict between the ideas of this group and the Spanish government would cause the exile of José M. Heredia (1803–39), the expulsion of José A. Saco (1797–1879), and the closing of the Cuban Academy of Literature. As Raimundo Lazo wrote, "this generation divides its efforts between the first revolutionary attempts at political liberty and the heroic work toward improving the nation's habits." [2] Products of this generation were the great poetry of Heredia, the systematic and enlightening criticism of Domingo del Monte (1804–53), and the concern for political, economic, and social problems in the essay of Saco. It is significant that the principal journalistic organ of this generation, the *Revista bimestre cubana* (1831), was the first to publish within Cuba an article on the slave traffic, examined from the political, social, and economic point of view.[3]

I   Félix Tanco: *Petrona y Rosalía* (1838)

Félix Manuel Tanco y Bosmoniel and Juan Francisco Manzano, whose texts constitute the first attempt to portray the blacks within the framework of antislavery literature, fully reflect the concern with abolition that is an essential note of their generation. Tanco, the author of *Petrona y Rosalía* (1838), was born in Bogotá in 1797, but he was brought to Cuba at the age of twelve and always considered himself a Cuban. In 1828, he was appointed postmaster of Matanzas, where he was director of the newspaper *La aurora* (1829) and an active member of the literary *tertulias* that were held in the years 1834–36 at the home of his intimate friend Domingo del Monte. When the humanist del Monte went back to Havana, he kept up a valuable correspondence with the writer from Matanzas, which may be found in the seventh volume of the famous critic's *Centón epistolario*. An active separatist and an ardent abolitionist, Tanco took part in several conspiracies and, after the bloody events of 1844, had to exile himself to the United States, where he published several pamphlets defending Cuban independence. He died in New York on 31 October 1871. Besides being a storywriter and political polemicist, he wrote some poems, which were published in *Rimas americanas* (1833).[4]

In a letter dated 20 August 1838, informing del Monte of the completion of *Petrona y Rosalía,* Tanco develops his ideas about what the Cuban novel ought to be. It should be a reflection of the society, presenting "the contrasts of the two colors of our population." In fact, what Tanco is proposing is the basic plan of the abolitionist novel, to present "the Negroes and the whites working on each other, corrupting each other even in the least important aspects of life, in such a way that in the white man we see the Negro and in the Negro the white."[5]

At the outset, he mentions the absence of the black character in the literary productions of the period, explaining this absence as a result of fear, scrupulosity, or revulsion: "Until now, it seems there has been and is fear or scruples or revulsion against presenting Negroes on the stage or in the novel beside whites the way they are in the census lists, and as if we weren't really united, but grafted onto each other, amalgamated like any pharmaceutical mixture."[6]

According to Tanco, the black must appear in the novel or theater of Cuba, for without him the portrayal of the country would be incomplete because it would fail to show the cause of the moral corruption of the white man—slavery: "I think the young men who are writing novelettes today are not hitting the mark when they describe lovemaking and gallantry among those of their own class or color, when they describe the corruption of this class without any reminder at all of the slaves who have such a strong role in this corruption: they hardly even dare write the word *bocabajo* [face-down]" [7]

Besides, as the author himself has tried to demonstrate in *Petrona y Rosalía,* Cuban fiction should be "a horribly true picture of our society and of our private customs," in which the slave is not reduced to a "ridiculous character, when slaves are not that"; in which "there is much dialogue and the author speaks only when necessary," and especially without being "muzzled." The blacks, he says, should express themselves in clear Spanish "as the creoles really speak it." [8]

In the same letter, Tanco notes the subversive character of his *Escenas cubanas,* and as he confesses the influence of Balzac he senses the destiny of all the abolitionist literature of the island: the impossibility of its publication because of the reformist and clearly revolutionary tone that provides its power:

> You must know that the idea of writing these *Escenas cubanas* does not originate with me; that accursed Balzac inspired it and encouraged it with his French ones, and I have such anxiety about the depiction that I can't set myself to the task. I presume that this is not publishable here, and that troubles me. But I swear that since I still want to write stories, I shall get together a volume and publish it in the United States, and then I'll hand it out free to as many people as I can. [9]

Tanco proposed to gather together under the title *Escenas cubanas* or *Escenas de la vida privada en la isla de Cuba* a collection of short novels in which he would describe the "customs and only the customs" of the period. [10] He planned three novels: *Petrona y Rosalía,* written in 1838 and published in 1925; [11] the *Hombre misterioso,* also edited in 1838, whose whereabouts is unknown; and the "Historia de Francisco," which he described in a letter sent to del Monte on 4 September 1838:

I have in mind another story, "Historia de Francisco." This is the story of a little twelve-year-old Negro taken out of the *barracón* when the *barracones* were right opposite the public mall and the African trade was carried out freely. With this little black Francisco I'm going to go into all the corners of the houses from the palace to the hovel and bring it all out into public view—or public shame.[12]

We don't know whether this story ever developed beyond this embryonic state, but we can see from what Tanco says that it follows the same general lines as another abolitionist text, the novel *Francisco* by Anselmo Suárez y Romero.

On the other hand, we know that Tanco did finish *Hombre misterioso,* although our knowledge of this text is limited to the account he provided to del Monte: "It is the aristocracy that is punished in *Petrona y Rosalía,* and in *Hombre misterioso,* the second story, it is the middle class. Everybody gets thoroughly dressed down and exposed to public shame; you'll see in *Hombre misterioso* how I depict our country priests." [13]

Petrona y Rosalía was finished in July 1838; its publication in December 1925 was a matter of pure chance. The original manuscript was in the hands of José R. García, a Cuban who had lived in Buenos Aires for more than fifty years, and he turned it over to the well-known bibliographer Carlos M. Trelles, who was visiting the Argentine capital as Cuban delegate to an inter-American conference toward the end of 1924. The diligent Trelles succeeded in having this curious manuscript published in the journal *Cuba contemporánea.*

In an extensive prologue to the story, Tanco outlines and expresses more clearly his ideas about the Cuban novel, ideas he had already communicated to Domingo del Monte. His basic idea is the necessity of including the black in any novel that proposes to depict Cuban customs: "The author of these *Escenas de la vida privada en la isla de Cuba* has thought and still thinks that no description or picture of Cuban customs will ever be perfect or complete if it does not include the slaves who have such a principal part in it." [14]

Nor should the author forget that these depictions should be "faithful" to the "profoundly corrupted" customs they describe. Thus, the function of the novelist is that of the "curious observer" who, "copying meticulously the society in which he lives," must "depict and criticize bad or ridiculous social habits." As can be seen, this is a romantic *costumbrismo* with eighteenth-century overtones, which, because it emphasizes exactness of detail without striving for melodramatic effects, verges on so-called realism.

Petrona y Rosalía, known also as *El niño Fernando,* is a long story in which dialogue predominates, although dialogue is not the only form of expression, as the prologue seems to imply (259). It recounts the sexual relations of the black Petrona with her master Don Antonio and of Rosalía, their mulatto offspring, with the "boy" Fernando, apparently a descendant of the white gentleman. Max Henríquez Ureña and Juan J. Remos y Rubio are wrong in claiming that the subject of incest is a point of coincidence between Tanco's story and *Cecilia Valdés* by Cirilo Villaverde.[15] In *Petrona y Rosalía,* there is in fact no incestuous relationship: Fernando is not the son of Don Antonio but the illegitimate offspring of his wife, Doña Concepción, and her lover, the marquis of Casanova (284). The parallel that does exist between these novels, however, is the repetition of the sexual experience of the black mother in the mulatto daughter, which produces a series of concubinages and crossbreedings, one of the central themes of the abolitionist novel.

Tanco's intention, more than an attempt to penetrate the black character and express it literarily, was to offer us a picture of the corruption experienced by the Cuban family, men and women, on account of slavery.

> If the family is the basis of civil society, what sort of society will ours be, and what kind of citizens will be reared among us when brute force has set up its throne against morality and justice right in the heart of the family, and where it is then necessary to have an executioner and all his instruments of oppression and torture in order to maintain its power? [259]

The role of the black in Tanco's story is thus reduced to that of explaining a phenomenon. The white, from his tenderest childhood, can exercise all manner of abuses of power over the black: the slave is a simple, defenseless plaything in the omnipotent hands of the master. Thus, the black in Cuban society has been reduced to the category of a thing; and as such she forms part of Tanco's story.

Thus, Tanco sees the black protagonist as a function of the white character. What he finally offers us, more than the vision of the black people, is the system of exploitation imposed on them. It would be futile to search in *Petrona y Rosalía* for differential ethnic features, to delve for the authentic psychology of the black woman and her mulatto daughter. What we note constantly are the reactions of the slaves to the actions of the masters. We could say that Tanco does not notice the difference between the black character and the institution of slavery. For this author, slave and black mean the same thing.

The external view of an elemental and stereotyped psychology and of absolutely passive behavior is the essential feature to be found in the creation of these two black women, Petrona and her daughter Rosalía. The former, after having been raped by her master Don Antonio, is condemned by his wife to the sugar mill—that is, to the slaves' hell. We don't know what the black woman feels on this tragic occasion; we know only that "The Negro had no choice but to be still and obey and resign herself to going off to the terrible refinery where she was faced with work, torture, and death" (263).

Doña Concepción saw to it that Petrona received the normal treatment for slaves at the sugar mill: "But since the señora suspected this willful omission of her husband's, she sent a letter on her own to the mayoral, telling him to cut off Petrona's chignon, to put her into a rough shirt, and to give her fifty lashes. No sooner said than done. The order was carried out to the letter" (263).

Such treatment did not keep the black woman from giving birth to Rosalía: "Petrona's natural robustness, like that of all her race, made her triumph over the work and bad treatment she had undergone for three months, at the end of which she gave birth to a girl, no, not a girl, but a mulatto, to whom she gave the name Rosalía" (263).

As we can see, the vision of the specific black character is obscured by the racial prejudice the author expresses without realizing it—the idea of the physical strength that makes the black woman able to withstand all manner of hard labor and bad treatment. Thus, Petrona is a sort of carnival doll, and the thing to stress, more than her reaction at this point, is the reaction of the master, Don Antonio, upon receiving word of the birth of his own daughter: "Señor Pantaleón, the foreman, told this news to Don Antonio as if he were reporting the dropping of a calf or of a pig because it represented an increment in the property of the master" (263). In fact, the "master" didn't even alter his expression and "the unhappy Petrona was to continue living at the mill, cutting cane and undergoing hard work and deprivations with a mulatto daughter" (264). The deformation of sensitivity that slavery produces in the white slaveholder—the basic concern of Tanco in these stories—is what determines this episode.

This deformation depends on an educative process that the author illustrates in his description of the "child" Fernandito. A very important part of the story is his "upbringing," especially as regards his behavior toward the unfortunate blacks. One of his favorite games involved striking the slave Julián with a whip: "the mother, always in fear of a tantrum, would call Julián and make him get onto his knees so that her dear little son could whip him as much as he cared to; the whippings ended up tickling Julián because his little master was all of ten years old" (265).

Thirteen years later, the "child" Fernandito has become a despotic and arrogant young man, and the little mulatto girl is now full of "the grace peculiar to the women of her class, especially in her black eyes with long eyelashes full of a seductive liveliness that the weight of servitude could never deaden, as long as she lived" (268). Doña Concepción, "taken with her as she might be with a jewel to adorn her house in Havana, resolved to take her along on account of her well-endowed face, her beautiful eyes, and her graceful body" (268). Rosalía is this typical young mulatto woman who will awaken the libidinous desires of the young white man.

When Don Antonio dies of apoplexy, his offspring takes over the functions of the master in every sense. Indeed, Fernandito rapes the mulatto woman, who becomes pregnant. At that time, Doña Concepción discovers that Rosalía is the daughter of her dead husband. "However, she didn't get upset about this matter [the relationship between the boy and the mulatto woman], remembering that Fernando was not the son of Don Antonio but the marques of Casanova" (284). There was no incest, but the rich woman could not bear the thought of having a mulatto grandchild. So, in order "to see whether she could free Don Fernando from having a black child and herself a black grandchild, for such a thought made her shudder with blushing" (284), Doña Concepción had recourse to an abortive medicine, which had no effect on Rosalía because of her strong constitution. She was condemned to the mill where she was reunited with her mother, and the second cycle of crossbreeding was completed.

As we see from this resumé of the plot, we have here the framework of a novel, which, although undeveloped, shows us all the typical motifs of the Cuban abolitionist narrative. That was Tanco's intention—to draw up an outline of the plot and later to develop it. As he tells his friend del Monte in a letter written in Matanzas 28 August 1838, "it was natural that you consider my novel about Petrona and Rosalía a rough draft, because when I wrote it I did not intend to show details and depict personal qualities. . . . As it turns out, what I have written is the outline of the plot of each novel so as to show *customs* and only *customs;* later I'll do the rest as you want it and it should be." [16]

These customs are, of course, those of the slave society this author is fighting, and so in this "plot outline" the story, the basic topics, and the methods of the Cuban abolitionist novel are already present. First, the story is arranged around the family group of the slave owner, with the possible repetition of two cycles of concubinage in consecutive generations of whites and blacks; in this way, the author brings out the role of slavery in the corruption and deformation of sensibility. Second, a typology is established: on the one hand, we have the master, the mistress, and the child (with an Oedipal relationship between child and mother), and on the other, the black or mulatto slave. Thus, a curious triangle is created in which it will be the mother who helps the son obtain sexual gratification with the black woman. Third, the plot is developed in two different settings, the city and the country, the first associated with the black's happiness, the second with her sad fortune. Fourth, the black character— the slave—is reduced to the status of a thing, an adornment of the large urban residence, or of a "whelp," a sugar-making machine in the mill; but in both cases she is a passive soul whose behavior is a product of the velleities of the slaveholder. To these constants, which can vary in detail but not essentially, add the fact that these narratives are intended as social documents or testimonies. *Sab* (1841) by Gertrudis Gómez de Avellandea is the only abolitionist novel that does not make use of these creative coordinates.

II   Juan F. Manzano: *Apuntes autobiográficos*

It is very strange that the *Apuntes autobiográficos* (1839) by Juan Francisco Manzano, a text that gives us the inner view of slavery and the black, is so similar in its depiction of the slave to the passive characterization we have already observed in *Petrona y Rosalía* and shall see repeated in *Francisco* by Anselmo Suárez y Romero. Here again we see the slaves reduced to adornments or instruments for agricultural production, transported back and forth by the white owners, without any evidence of individually motivated behavior as long as they remain enslaved. This doesn't mean that the slaves do not rebel against the unjust system that oppresses them, or that they do not even try to run away. We just want to point out that Manzano, like Tanco, is more concerned with painting the institution of slavery than with depicting the human being who is forced to suffer under it. Thus, the slave is perceived as sort of a receptacle in which all the inequities of the system are concentrated. Both the white novelist and the black poet want to move their readers, and in order to do this, they depict the socioeconomic organization that subjugates the black. The *Apuntes autobiográficos* by Manzano are written with openly abolitionist intent.

Juan Francisco Manzano (1797–1854) was born the slave of the marqués of Jústiz and Santiago, carrying the name of his masters, as was the custom then. Until he was eleven, when the marchioness died, he had a relatively happy childhood; but under the new mistress, the marchioness of Prado Ameno, he began to experience all the horrors of slavery.

In his function as page, he was able to attend dramatic performances, which gradually awoke in him an interest in poetry. Before he could read or write, he composed *décimas* in his mind. In 1821, he received special permission to publish a collection of his *Poesías líricas* (slaves were not normally permitted to publish). In several newspapers in Havana and Matanzas, other works of his began to come to light, and in the literary *tertulia* of Domingo del Monte his famous sonnet "Mis treinta años" was read. In 1836, at the instigation of del Monte and Ignacio Valdés Machuca, a campaign was started to raise funds to buy the slave poet's manumission, and the following year, 1837, the 850 pesos exacted by his owner were paid. From then on, Manzano wrote little: he published his mediocre tragedy *Zafira* in 1842, and he finally stopped writing after the tragic events of 1844, which caused him to be imprisoned and cost the unfortunate Plácido his life.[17]

In 1835, the restless and curious del Monte had suggested to Manzano that he write the memoirs of his slave life;[18] and this resulted in the *Apuntes autobiográficos,* finished in 1839. According to José L. Franco, they were divided into two parts: "the first was entrusted to Suárez y Romero, who made a corrected copy for Richard R. Madden; the second got out of the hands of [Ramón de] Palma, and was never found again."[19] Madden, the ardent antislavery British commissioner to the slave-trade arbitration tribunal, succeeded in getting out of Cuba the copy Suárez had given him and in publishing it, along with other works of Manzano, in a volume entitled *Poems by a Slave in the Island of Cuba, recently liberated. Translated from the Spanish by R. R. Madden, M.D., with the history of the Early Life of the Negro Poet, written by himself, to which are prefixed two pieces descriptive of Cuban Slavery and the Slave-traffic* (London, 1840). The original manuscript of the first part, in Manzano's own handwriting, kept in the National Library of Havana, was published in 1937 under the title *Autobiografía.*

The *Apuntes autobiográficos* of Juan F. Manzano narrate clearly and directly the first thirty-three years of his life, in chronological order, although not always exactly. As Max Henríquez Ureña has written: "His narration is so ingenuous and spontaneous that he doesn't even stop to comment on the bitter experiences he has endured or to add qualifying adjectives; he is doubtless confident that this exposition of facts says more, much more, than any commentary; and he succeeds in leaving upon the reader the impression of an authentic emotion."[20]

In fact, Manzano's narration is a series of punishments and troubles from which emerges the image of the slave as a poor, passive being, subject to the whim, the insanity, and the criminal violence of his masters and his foremen. This text, which brought tears to Suárez y Romero as he copied it and which possibly influenced his *Francisco,* is a unique document of the life of the black under slavery. Suárez's commentary to del Monte is especially moving: "My heart, which identifies itself so closely with the misfortunes of this kind of children, who because of having been born slaves, get up in tears, eat their meals in tears, and perhaps even dream in tears—you can imagine how much my heart ached as I copied Manzano's story."[21]

Manzano, for his part, in a letter written to del Monte on 25 June 1835, describes the pains of his slave life in a pathetic resumé of the story:

> a picture of so many adversities seems but a bulky record of deceits, and besides, from such a tender age the whips made me aware of my humble status. . . . remember, your mercy, as you read, that I am a slave and the slave is a dead being before his master; do not lose sight of what I have gained; consider me a martyr, and you'll find that the whips that mutilated my flesh, still unformed, will never vilify your affectionate servant.[22]

We can see in the above letter that Manzano is in fact establishing the basic elements that will make up the abolitionist narrative. On the one hand, we have the "picture of so many adversities"; on the other, the characterization of the black protagonist as a "dead being before his master." From the joining of these two, we have the condition of "martyrdom." The poet himself perceived the novelistic potential of these elements for that period, for in the letter written on 29 September 1835, he writes del Monte that he will reserve "the most interesting happenings of my life for the day when, seated in a corner of my country, tranquil, assured of my safety and subsistence, I may write a truly Cuban novel." [23]

We have here what we might call the raw materials for a novel; but these materials bring with them the problem of the repetitive and therefore tedious nature of the episodes narrated. This element even makes difficult an attractive organization of the *Apuntes autobiográficos:* "If I tried to make an exact resumé of the story of my life, it would be a repetition of similar events; for since I was thirteen or fourteen, my life has been a series of penances, lockups, whippings, and anguishes." [24] And this is indeed what is narrated in this curious document.

As Manzano describes his life as a page to the marchioness of Prado Ameno—a life that didn't allow him time even for eating or other physiological functions—we see beneath a certain ingenuous grace in this passage the tragically inhuman condition of the slave.

> We spent five years in Matanzas, and there it was my job to sweep and clean as much as I could at dawn, before anyone else was up. When that was finished, I sat down at my mistress' door

so as to be there when she awoke. And then, wherever she went, I went like a little lapdog, but with my arms crossed. When they ate dinner or supper, I took care to take everything they all left, and I had to manage to gobble it up before they got up from the table.[25]

Whenever he didn't behave like a proper little lapdog and acted freely like any boy his age, he was punished with a refined and barbarous cruelty. "I suffered for the least boyish mischief, closed up in a coalbin. . . . after hard whippings, I was shut up under orders that anyone who gave me a single drop of water would be severely punished. This penance was so frequent that not a week passed without my suffering this kind of punishment two or three times." [26]

But being sent to the sugar mill is the big punishment, and on the sugar plantation the "penance" has elements of real tragedy, because there it is witnessed by the poet's mother, from whom he lives separated when he is in Havana or Matanzas. The description of a "facedown" punishment, in its stark pathos, reveals all the human and moral degradation that the slave regime imposes on slaves and masters.

Don Silvester was the name of the young overseer. Driving me with the whip, he came upon my mother, who, following the impulses of her heart, had come to crown my misfortunes. When she saw me she tried to ask me what I had done. The overseer, making her keep still, wanted to get her out of the way without hearing any begging or supplication. Irritated because they had made him get up at that hour, he raised his hand and struck my mother with the manatee whip. I felt that blow in my heart. In a flash I had cried out and changed from a meek lamb into a lion. My mother and I were taken and put into the same place. We both groaned as one. . . . Dawn had hardly broken when two "counteroverseers" and the overseer came and got us, each one of the Negroes taking his "prey" to the sacrifice. . . . Indecorously, four Negroes grabbed her and threw her to the ground to whip her. For her sake I bore it all, but at the first crack of the whip . . . I was on the point of losing my life at the hands of Silvester.[27]

The import of the above citation justifies its length, for now we are dealing with the description of a typical theme of the abolitionist novel. The *Apuntes autobiográficos* are in fact a constant repetition of this kind of scene: the facedown punishments and other physical chastisements of the slave are designed to convert them into the "dead beings" that the poet had spoken of, an excellent, graphic expression to define the legal and literary personality of the enslaved black.

But we note, too, the rebelliousness and the sense of dignity of the slave—two elements that will be part of the formation of the slave protagonist. In spite of the regime that tyrannizes him, he remains a man and reacts as a man to the stimuli of his master and his bailiffs. Thus, we can see that the extraliterary intent of the abolitionist writers is to emphasize the human state of their black characters, in reply to a society that believes the opposite. We see this phenomenon clearly in Manzano, in Villaverde, in Suárez, and in Avellaneda; and on account of it there is an almost complete absence of differentiating ethnic elements in their slave characters. Let us take a look, for example, at how Juan Francisco Manzano describes the crisis of his adolescence:

> From about the age of thirteen or fourteen, the happiness and vivacity of my disposition and the talkativeness of my lips— called a golden mouth—all changed into a certain melancholy, which as time passed became characteristic of me. Music delighted me, but without knowing why, I cried, and I enjoyed this consolation when I needed to cry; I always looked for solitude to give vent to my sorrows. I cried, but I didn't groan, nor did my heart become tight; I just remained in a state of incurable depression until daylight.[28]

Chronic melancholy and depression, love of music, of weeping, and of solitude, are the elements of a personality very much in vogue in that period and in that country—the personality is surprisingly romantic and therefore disappointing to the researcher who is looking for "primitivism" and "Africanness." Of course, we cannot forget that Manzano was a black creole with some cultural background, which, although rudimentary, was not much inferior to that of Plácido, for example. On the other hand, he was subject to the influence of men of letters like del Monte and his last master, Don Nicolás de Cárdenas, to whom the marchioness of Prado Ameno had "rented him out." From Don Nicolás he learned reading and developed a fondness for studying.

> Don Nicolás (de Cárdenas) . . . loved me not as a slave but as a son. . . . when I saw that as soon as he was up, when it was barely light and before doing anything else, he was preparing his desk, chair, and books to dedicate himself to study, I gradually took on the same habits, so that I, too, began to devote myself to study. Poetry, in all the undertakings of life, ministered to me with verses analogous to my situation.[29]

But to search for Manzano's "Africanness" in these *Apuntes auto-biográficos* would be to court disappointment. Our slave poet is black, but he is a Cuban black. Placed in the cultural process of that country and responding to the stimuli of his social environment, he is a product of the historical circumstances into which he was born. Manzano never thought about an impossible return trip to the African continent; his fatherland, even though it had enslaved him, was Cuba. Besides, his desire was always to strengthen his ties with this land, because he felt he belonged to it. Thus, as we have noted, the novel he projects is Cuban, not African or even Negro. There is clearly here a strong desire for integration. His fond hope was that some day he would find himself "seated in a corner of *my country,* tranquil, assured of my safety and my subsistence," where "I may write a truly *Cuban* novel." We find that the italics, which are ours, are an obvious corroboration of what we are saying.

Chapter Four

The Romantic Abolitionist Novel

As Max Henríquez Ureña has said, "the Cuban novel is the legitimate offspring of *costumbrista* literature";[1] hence, the presence of the black protagonist in the Cuban narrative is practically as old as the genre. Narrative prose had appeared in Cuba in the form of a story with an Indian theme—*Matanzas y Yumurí* (1837) by Ramón de Palma (1812–60)[2]—and in the next year Félix Tanco y Bosmoniel made the first attempt at antislavery fiction. But it was the first group of Cuban romantics who fully developed the narrative possibilities of the black, slave or free, the mulatto, and the institution of slavery— still maintaining the creative coordinates I have outlined.

Members of the first generation of romantics on the island were Anselmo Suárez y Romero (1818–78), author of *Francisco;* Cirilo Villaverde (1812–94), author of *Cecilia Valdés;* and Gertrudis Gómez de Avellaneda (1814–73), who in a period of youthful exaltation had written *Sab*. To these works, which gave Cuba primacy in the American abolitionist novel, we should add the novel *Romualdo: Uno de tantos* by Francisco Calcagno (1827–1903), who really belongs to the second generation of Cuban romantics.[3]

The two generations of Cuban romantics, corresponding to the first group of Spanish-American romantics, according to the generational outline set up by José Juan Arrom,[4] were to witness and suffer a progressive intensification of the climate of political tension that had begun toward the second decade of the nineteenth century and that reached a violent crisis with the outbreak of the Ten Years' War (1868–78). Cuba lost its status as an overseas province as a result of the Royal Order of 21 March 1834, and beginning with the government of Gen. Miguel Tacón (1834–38), it was made a European colony with a special policy for native-born Cubans.[5] That explains why the abolitionist narratives written there could not be published until much later, whereas Avellaneda was free to turn her novel *Sab* over to the Madrid press. Literarily, these two groups were to take part in the triumph and decadence of romanticism, the second group initiating a reform of the movement, especially in poetry. This process of surpassing the romantic aesthetic was suspended when the revolution of 1868 broke out.[6]

Thus, the Cuban abolitionist novel was born in a tense and charged political atmosphere and a period of strong compulsion from the mother country, but we cannot properly characterize it as anti-Spanish. The only instance of anti-Spanish sentiment among these narrators shows itself, curiously, when Avellaneda is affecting pure Castilian blood, although it is a historical anti-Spanishism and follows the literary fashion of the period. In Suárez, in Villaverde, and in Calcagno, there was clear recognition of the fact that breaking the ties with the mother country was not sufficient grounds for altering the "moral" constitution of the country, according to the expression of the period. The important thing was a change in the institutions— chiefly, the abolition of the slave system, the basis of Cuban society and of her economy. These texts were really revolutionary for their period; there is no paternalism of any kind in them, and the thought that must be inferred is that the colonial, owner of slaves, is himself a slave and that in order to achieve his own political independence he must first free his slaves. Thus, the characterization of the black protagonists has a double purpose: to underline their basic human condition, and to point up the corruption of the slave society. From the first, underplaying basically differentiating ethnic features, came the image of the slave hero; from the second—centered in sexual abuse and crossbreeding—came the figure of the mulatto woman, variable in her psychological characterization but always perceived as the propitiatory victim of this society of force. That is why G. R. Coulthard could write, "The Cuban abolitionist novel is not purely anti-Spanish propaganda literature."[7]

I   Anselmo Suárez y Romero: *Francisco*

The absence of differentiating ethnic features, seen in Tanco and in Manzano, is noticeable also in *Francisco: El ingenio; o, Las delicias del campo* by Anselmo Suárez y Romero. This novel does contain a few elements that characterize the soul of the black, but the general impression produced by reading it doesn't differ greatly from that produced by Manzano's autobiography. This is due not only to the possible influence of the slave poet on the Havana novelist but also to the fact that both texts were written with one idea in mind: to supply Richard R. Madden with illustrative documents for his abolitionist propaganda.

At the instigation of Domingo del Monte, from whom Madden had requested "a few compositions by Cuban authors for the purpose of determining the state of opinion about the trade and slaves," [8] Suárez y Romero began writing *Francisco* at the end of 1838 at his home in Puentes Grandes. The following year he moved with his family to the Surinam refinery in the district of Güines, and "from the country he sent the rough draft to José Zacarías González del Valle, for him to correct and copy." The clean copy, made by this intimate friend of the poet, was sent to del Monte, who thought the title *El ingenio; o, Las delicias del campo* [The refinery; or, the delights of the country] would be more appropriate because of its irony.[9] This was the manuscript that del Monte turned over to Madden on the eve of his departure from Cuba, although the British commissioner never managed to publish it in the "Album de composiciones negreras" he was planning to edit in London.[10] The author himself didn't know what happened to the copy given to the English consul. Because of its decidedly abolitionist affirmations, the novel could be circulated only in handwritten form among the intimate members of the del Monte atheneum. In 1859, when Suárez was editing a *Colección de artículos,* he wanted to include with them some "fragments" of *Francisco,* but the "censor threw them out when he had barely read the first paragraphs." [11] The work was published successfully in New York in 1880 shortly after the death of the author, through the efforts of the Cuban historian Vidal Morales y Morales.

As Mario Cabrera Saquí had pointed out, Suárez's purpose "was to offer a true picture of the slave question, to provide documentation for Madden." [12] No better person could have been chosen from del Monte's tertulia than this author, because of his direct acquaintance with rural slavery, in particular that of the sugar plantations. In a letter from the country dated 15 March 1839, he commented to del Monte:

> And in vain does one leave the refinery and move to other plantations, for everywhere there are slaves and masters, which is to say that everywhere there groans a race of unfortunate men under the power of another more fortunate one, which takes advantage, inhumanely, of its toiling and sweating. Nevertheless, since you commissioned a novel in which the events would concern whites and blacks, and since I have begun it, I have acquired such an eagerness to observe the excesses of the former and the suffering of the latter, such a pleasure in studying the customs that grow out of slavery, strange and infinitely varied customs, that I am not bored but pleased by my sojourn here, where I can gather information and argument with which to write some day. [13]

Francisco is, therefore, a testimonial document. The clear abolitionist character of the novel is implicit in the narration; it is a result that the reader naturally deduces. However, upon occasion, such as when he is developing the topic of slavery's corruption of family customs, the author openly expresses not only his abolitionism but also the principle of equality of the races, which had been trampled underfoot by the institution of slavery: "it seems that slavery has spread through our atmosphere a poison that annihilates the most philanthropic ideas and leaves in its trail only hate and disdain for the unfortunate black people." [14]

This cancer, produced by slavery, makes for constant conflict between whites and blacks, oppressors and oppressed. The privileged ones have to live with whip in hand to maintain the superiority they enjoy: "with Negroes, condescension is worth nothing; it is lost on them, and it is the masters who suffer; skin them alive, handle them with the switch, with kicks and blows, like mules or dogs, and you'll be served well; they'll be smarter than a lynx" (45–46).

In the whites, there is an attempt to justify this attitude by means of a topical rationalization: the supposed animality and insensitivity of the blacks: "They are descended from the apes, let it not be doubted; notice their big mouths, their flat noses, their flat foreheads, their kinky hair, their idleness, their slowness, their slovenliness, their bestiality, and their ingratitude toward everyone" (46).

On the other hand, a righteous rebellion against the white oppressor is suggested in the novel, although in a veiled and offhand manner, so as not to damage the image the author is trying to project; the rebellion takes the form of rising up, fleeing, turning against the overseer, and even planning sabotage in the bagasse houses and the mills (123).

The abolitionism in *Francisco* is manifested in the relationships established between the master and his agents on the one hand and the slaves on the other; in the infernal situation created by the hard work and long hours in the mill; and in the bloody punishments imposed on the hero of the story. Thus, even Señora Mendizábal realizes how roughly she has treated Dorotea and Francisco as a result of becoming "overexcited" (107); the author gives precise details of the terrible workday in a sugar mill during the grinding season, a day that never ends; and he describes in all their sadistic particulars the sufferings the slave has to undergo:

> Nor did the young fellow [Ricardo] forget to have him suffer nine days of early-morning whippings.... Francisco received three hundred and five lashes in the short space of ten days, and as a result he was so debilitated that he lay motionless on the bench; the overseer had left his buttocks lacerated with open wounds, pitiful to see. But he wasn't satisfied with that; seeing that he couldn't go out to the fields, he tried to martyr him by whatever other means he could. Among those his cruelty brought to mind, none seemed so appropriate as to rub right into those wounds and cuts, six times a day until the blood spurted from them, dry corn straw moistened with that terrible mixture of whiskey, urine, salt, and tobacco used by our overseers for a severe punishment. That was a pleasure, a rather innocent recreation. [80–81]

Here Suárez shows one of the psychological characteristics of the "mill master": the perversion of the sex instinct to sadism, a feature already observed in some characters of Tanco and Manzano.

We see this characteristic here in Ricardo, and it will appear again in Leonardo de Gamboa.

Francisco is the story of the sad love affair of Francisco, the calash driver, an African black, and Dorotea, the handmaid, a colonial mulatto woman of "rare beauty" (55). When they are not allowed to· marry, they maintain a secret relationship, the fruit of which is a little girl, Lutgarda. Francisco is punished by being sent to the sugar mill, and Dorotea is condemned to service as a laundress in the home of a French woman. In the sugar mill, the former calash driver is subjected to all kinds of physical and mental torture by the "playboy" Ricardo, who desires the mulatto woman. To ease her lover's punishment, Dorotea gives herself to the young master. Francisco, in despair, commits suicide, "and the mulatto woman, pining away little by little, died after a few years" (177).

To be sure, this account of such a melancholy love affair, and especially the reactions of the protagonists, smacks of romanticism. The lovers, especially Francisco, are perceived as cultured people. Even the "despair" of the black calash driver has the romantic stamp, although we must agree that its external manifestation has not. However, the means of suicide the hero chooses—hanging—was not ordinarily used by the African "tribal" blacks, who used the terrible method of "swallowing their tongues," causing death by asphyxiation. Generally, in the characterization of Francisco we can see the traits of the romantic hero. Even Suárez y Romero was aware of this. Replying to a criticism by del Monte, he commented:

> I was trying to paint the Negro slave; and who, upon finding himself groaning under the terrifying and irritating yoke of serfdom could be so docile, so calm, endowed with such angelic and saintly manners as he? . . . Francisco is a phenomenon, a very singular exception. . . . So it was that from the time I began writing, I got angrier and angrier with the whites as I went on describing their misconduct, and since it is in my character, I must confess, to tolerate with patience the misfortunes of this Vale of Tears, I ended up endowing Francisco with that same Christian resignation and meekness. That is the reason for my mistake.[15]

Francisco is therefore an exceptional person, not the typical product of the slave system. He is "docile," "calm" and full of "angelic and saintly manners," as was the kind Anselmo Suárez y Romero. Thus, the character is autobiographical as far as his psychology and moral conduct are concerned. Moreover, this text illustrates a very great difficulty faced by novelists of the period, one they generally had to overcome if they attempted to express the physical and social reality of Hispanic America. The Cubans and the *criollistas*, for example, were trying to give literary form to an environment and its inhabitants that were very different from their own cultural backgrounds. Even in Suárez y Romero, we can see an explicit rejection of the social values that shaped him and a sentimental identification with that other world to which he is trying to give literary expression. The paradox and the error occur because the author is caught in his own social environment and cannot rid himself of the points of view that characterize it; so he attributes white morality and other values of Western civilization to his character, and he describes African music from the point of view of cultivated European rhythms. As a result, the identification referred to above is rather an assimilation of black attributes to white ones, in which the author remains practically immobile. There is no movement to the other side: there is only a contemplation of it from the author's own ego. And, of course, that ego—white and Occidental—shapes the one it wants to create. So Francisco becomes a contradictory character: a black with white ideals, which at that moment were those of romanticism. In fact, the protagonist is African only in name (he is a "mina," a native of the region now known as Nigeria) and in his faintly African features, which we shall analyze at an appropriate time. Francisco is an "Ethiopian," twenty-four years old—"since he had been carried off from Africa at the age of ten, it was easy for Señora Mendizábal to mold him as she wished" (52). At the beginning of the story, Suárez depicts him as a man with a remarkable stature, graceful and elegant in his manner, walking around with his head high and "his jet black face gleaming all the more because of the pure white of his eyes and his teeth." The "beauty of Francisco" has double value, because his features "revealed the nobility and generosity of his heart" (53). He was of humble nature; "the smile and the melancholy look that spread a certain expression of sadness over his face even when some flash of joy came to his soul, and that plaintive way of talking, carried away everyone who knew him" (53). Francisco's innate morality "advanced more" when he heard the "maxims and holy counsel" of his mistress, and through his own efforts he learned to read and write, "laboring under all manner of inconveniences." To these skills and his "lively understanding," the protagonist added an extraordinary musical ability: "if we said that he sang 'El llanto,' exquisitely, we should give you an idea of the sweetness of his voice, of his grace and style, which caused the calash drivers to give him the nickname 'Golden Mouth' " (55). Manzano was also given that name by his fellow servants, as we've noted.

Finally, to complete this picture of idealized perfection, the character must have an acute awareness of his tragic destiny—being a slave—a destiny he will accept with resignation up until the moment he discovers that he cannot consummate his love. At that point, he will despair of his state, putting an end to his torments—also very romantically—by means of suicide. But before arriving at this tragic episode, Anselmo Suárez depicts Francisco as a "martyr of the faith":

> One burden afflicted him perennially: that of having slave status; a burden the privileges granted by his mistress could not ease; it could be extinguished only by death. He had resolved to suffocate this pain and torment, believing that if his suffering were known the burden would grow instead of being mitigated; his meek nature was in perfect harmony with the resignation of the Christian, the suffering of the stoic, the mark of an elevated soul that remains serene amidst the misfortunes that oppress it. Hence, that gloomy hue of his face, captivating and seductive, that shade used in representations of the martyrs of the faith. [53–54]

As the novel progresses, the romantic features of the protagonist are accentuated by the love element and by the tragic turn in his relationship with Dorotea. The slave becomes "authentically" sensitive, aware of his loneliness and helplessness, and for him nature is the only tranquilizing "balm." Francisco weeps with "muffled sobs" and "tears that flood his cheeks" (72) because of his mistress's ingratitude, the ferocity of the overseer, the ill will of Ricardo, the threats of the doctor, and the thousands of memories of Dorotea. At twilight, he gives himself over to "meditating on the griefs of the other Negroes" (77); at night he cannot get to sleep "because the silence and the solitude recall his misfortunes in all their magnitude"

(78). As his tears proliferate, we come to take Suarez's image literally: the slave "needs nothing else for his nurture" (89).

Nature is the only consolation for the poor black's wounded sensitivity. Thus, nature and the hero become identified with one another. In the Cuban landscape, Francisco finds appropriate surroundings for "lamenting his griefs" (90), besides the relief that the forest, "so much in accord with the state of his soul, poured into his wounds" (90). On the other hand, when he experiences the fleeting joy brought by the arrival of Dorotea at the mill, "he perceives everything as happy that afternoon, the water, the grass, the trees, the sky, and the birds" (172). This is clearly a romantic identification of the protagonist with tropical nature.

Although Francisco was exceptional—Ricardo intended to debase and disdain the calash driver, considering him equal to the other blacks on his estate (80)—we can find attitudes and features in the slave similar to those of the "tribal" black. For example, when Francisco is punished,, he becomes "dogged," a word the white masters and their agents used to describe the strength and forbearance of slaves subjected to the "facedowns" and other kinds of floggings: "But the Negro became dogged, like a highland boar, and he refused to tell any more; he bit the earth, he bit his thick lips, he bled from his mouth and ground his teeth" (44). On the estate, the calash driver had close relationships with other "mina" Africans, his "shipmates" (those who had come from the same part of Africa), as in fact was the custom among the mill workers. Finally, when Dorotea tells him about her disgrace, "He hid himself in the darkest part of the grove of trees, where he threw himself to the ground and rolled over and over as the tribal Negroes did when they were in despair, tearing his hair and biting the ground" (175).

Nevertheless, the essential image of Francisco is the romantic one with which Suárez closes his novel:

> Without father or mother or brothers or sisters or any relative, without friends; in Cuba, a land of whites; a slave, son of Africa and black; with an imagination ardent as the sun that warmed him when he was born; with a fine sensitivity; when he opened his eyes, and no longer wished to play childhood games, when he began to know his sad destiny, and one or two bitter tears rolled down his burning cheek in the silence and loneliness of

the night, where had he searched first for solace, who had wiped those tears ever since, if not Dorotea? But now, what was there left to make life pleasing for him? Everything, everything was lost! [176]

The female protagonist, although much less developed, shows the same romantic idealization. Dorotea, the seamstress and handmaid of Señora Mendizábal, is a colonial mulatto of "rare beauty, purity, and modesty" (55), the "angel—as we've seen—for whom Francisco longed in his sorrowful hours." In no way does she epitomize the sensual and voluptuous mulatto woman: her love is controlled by the stamp of fidelity and purity. The stain that tarnishes her purity results from the blindness of her mistress, who keeps her from "glimpsing any ray of hope" (59–60).

Her greatest sorrow was "the separation from what she loved most on Earth" (108). The licentious Ricardo's entreaties, promises, and threats were worthless, because "she was firm in her intention to keep her honor and be faithful to Francisco" (87). Therefore, she was willing to leave the city and go to the country to "work like other Negroes," in order to have "the sweet recompense of enjoying a few moments of happiness with him" (133). She prefers this life of suffering—but of purity, constancy, and honor—to the concubinage the "playboy" impudently proposes to her, no matter whether it brings her a certificate of freedom (145). She does not aspire to the white man's love, because she knows that racial prejudice will not permit him to offer her marriage, as the black man does (87). She is therefore very much aware of her status in society as a mulatto and a slave. When Ricardo, in an ecstasy of voluptuousness, tries to seduce her by saying, "Oh! I would give anything to be a Negro if it meant I could please you" (144), she replies with complete serenity: "The 'boy' mustn't even think about that. The 'boy' doesn't know the labors we are subjected to; that's why he talks that way" (144). Dorotea knows that she is one more victim of this society of compulsion.

Mario Cabrera Saqui has pointed to the influence of Bernardin de Saint-Pierre on the novel of Anselmo Suárez y Romero.[16] Indeed, a moving lyricism is evident in the story of these two people who love each other in such an ingenuous and passionate way and in the special role of nature, both aesthetically and in the sentiment that accompanies it, in Suárez y Romero's novel. But it should be pointed out that, if it is indeed true that the characterization of the two black protagonists follows the principles of the romantics, Suárez "succeeded in copying an interesting picture from reality,"[17] establishing a contrast between a truly paradisiacal tropical nature and the slave system in all its bloody cruelty. For this reason, the novel is conceived as one more example of the generational topic that Heredia had expressed so well: the beauties of the physical world in collision with the horrors of the moral one.

II   Cirilo Villaverde: *Cecilia Valdés*

A similar idea underlies *Cecilia Valdés* (1839); we include it in this chapter because in its definitive version of 1882 it is a product of the same ethical and aesthetic features that inform the earliest edition of the first part. Villaverde proudly proclaims himself "more than anything else, a realistic writer, in the artistic sense in which the word is currently used," [18] and elsewhere he declares that the "work which is now coming out in complete form does not contain the defects of language and style which were found in the first volume printed in Havana" (51). But the volume that appeared in New York in 1882 has, as Manuel de la Cruz has indicated, an "archaic character," animated as it is by an "antiquated kind of aesthetic." [19] This wise observation is corroborated by the author's own words in the prologue, where he declares: "I have not read a novel in 30 years, Scott and Manzoni being my only model for the various scenes in *Cecilia Valdés*" (50).

Thus, this novel is conceived with the double guidelines of the historical novel of romanticism and of the *costumbrismo* so in vogue in the Hispanic literature of the mid-nineteenth century. The story is of the immediate past, with a marked tone of allegation against the injustices of the colonial regime; and reality is depicted by the most primitive techniques—"I carried realism, as I understand it, to the point of presenting the principal characters of the novel with every hair and scar" (50). Villaverde does not succeed in disguising the essentially melodramatic elements that are the basis of the tale, adultery, incest, and assassination. These elements, the motive powers of the story, are clearly rooted in romanticism and are constantly used by Villaverde in his most scathing novels (for example, *El penitente,* 1844).

Cirilo Villaverde, as has been repeated so many times since Manuel de la Cruz pointed it out in 1885, proposed to denounce the many faults of the colonial administration—above all, "the political, moral, and social state of Cuban society in the period of 1812 to 1831"— by means of a "picture of vast dimensions" in which is included a study of "all classes and all their tendencies; they have all been called to justice and put into motion on the great stage." [20] This is why Enrique José Varona said that "*Cecilia Valdés* is the social history of Cuba." [21] It is indeed that: Villaverde's novel has become an important source of data for historians, as Loló de la Torriente proved in his study, *The Havana of Cecilia Valdés* (1946).

The author's desire to "make social history," which even leads him to note that "he has committed three anachronisms in the historical part of his novel" (549), transforms the work into a motley collection of episodes, many of which are unnecessary. It is "the prolixity of details" mentioned by Diego Vicente Tejera that slows "the progress of the action and makes the reading tedious, especially for the foreigner who, because he doesn't know Cuba, cannot consider them even so important as the Cuban may consider them." [22] And because the author is more intent on bringing the historical background into focus than on creating a small novelesque universe, the characters lose their definition and in many cases are lost in the course of the narration. Martín Morúa Delgado found this lack of force in the creation of the characters to be one of the fundamental deficiencies in *Cecilia Valdés.* "What really makes this novel weak," he said, "is the absence of a true character, for there is not one among so many personages. There are many types, indeed diverse types, but barely sketched; they frequently appear as murky figures, such as those that are lost in the dark background of a painting." [23] This is really a novel of customs and types; however, because of its constant tendency toward inventory and photographic description, it is but a step away from realism. As has been said, "it typifies par excellence the *costumbrista* novel of romanticism." [24]

Besides this antiquated aesthetic, the attitudes reflected in this novel place it in the first period of Cuban romanticism. Villaverde is an echo of the philanthropic ideas circulating among those who frequented del Monte's atheneum, ideas that were very outmoded when the first complete edition appeared in 1882. Morúa Delgado made this clear: "And in my opinion *Cecilia Valdés* owes its disapproval, shown by its lukewarm popularity, more to the conservative spirit that informs it than to its artistic imperfection." [25]

For Morúa Delgado, this attitude is reflected in the state of deformation in which Villaverde presents his characters; it is further revealed in the author's presentation of the black problem as he thinks the black character sees it.

Like Tanco's *Petrona y Rosalía*, *Cecilia Valdés* is the story of repeated concubinage and mixing of blood, the last relationship in the story being an incestuous one. We pass through different shades of blackness—real ethnic castes—until we come to Cecilia, a quadroon by blood, although apparently nearly white. Maria de Regla, the slave who has been her wet nurse, describes this crossbreeding process, a key to understanding the vicious circle Villaverde establishes in the black woman and the mulatto one: "Madalena, Negro like me, with a white man, had Seña Chepilla, a brown girl; Seña Chepilla, with another white man, had Seña Charito Alarcón, a light brown girl, and Seña Charito, with another white man, had Cecilia Valdés, a white girl" (448).

Departing from an inflexible moral criterion, Villaverde is denouncing with this fatal sequence the only practicable sexual relationship between the races in that period and the product derived from it, the mulatto. This one thought, implicit in the whole novel, is expressed openly in the proverb spoken by Seña Clara. This "experienced" mulatto woman, who has suffered many "irritations and deceptions" by whites, constantly repeats to the young mulatto women: "Each one with her each one" (321). For not following this line of conduct, Charo will end her days in an insane asylum and Cecilia in a jail in the same building, the Paula Hospital.

This fatal succession of sexual melodramas begins with Madalena Morales, "an old, squalid Negro woman, the picture of death, a dark skeleton" (62), who hardly appears in the story. María Josefa Alarcón, (called Chepilla), "brown" daughter of Madelena and a white man, is the typical dark mulatto woman: at forty, she is "of medium height, fleshy with a narrow waist, and bare rounded shoulders, a beautiful head, and thick, very curly hair" (59); at sixty, she has become copper-colored, she has a faded look, and the whole structure of her typical sensual beauty has collapsed. An intelligent woman, "as a young girl she had a comfortable life, she had some possessions, and she was on intimate terms with well-bred and mannerly people" (61); as an old woman, she makes an extravagant show of piety in order to "placate the anger of her invisible judge" (75). She has led a "wrathful" life, and because of it she still has an "irascible" nature and a constant obsession with the sins she has committed. She wants to use her acquaintance with life to help Cecilia avoid the errors she has fallen into. Her granddaughter must climb in the social scale of the colony by marrying a white: "You, on the contrary, are almost white and you can aspire to marrying a white. Why not? God made us, and you'll find out that a white even though poor is a good husband; a Negro or a mulatto isn't worth it, not even if he's a golden ox. I speak from experience" (78).

The girl learns the lesson very well. "My face would fall with shame if I married a Negro and had a throwback child," she will later say to her intimate friend Nemesia (322).

Chepilla was the typical image of mulatto beauty whose mixture of blood, a little enigmatic, lends her a special charm and a certain mystery. The essential features of her physical and psychological makeup—her beauty and sensuality and her indomitable character— as well as her desire to ascend in the ethnic composition of Cuban society and her belated repentance, all will be repeated in the daughter and the granddaughter. But in the story she functions as Cecilia's "mamita," taking into account the madness that attacked Rosario (Charo). In this sense, we could establish a parallel between Doña Rosa, who is presented in the novel as the typical example of the Cuban mother, and the old mulatto woman. It would be evident that they are not very different. Both Seña Josefa and the aristocratic countess of Casa Gamboa are concerned only for the happiness of their offspring, taking the term *happiness* in its most immediate and primitive sense. Both of them are religious; the practice of the cult becomes for both of them a kind of metaphysical inducement with which they expect to obtain heavenly favors. Thus Seña Josefa, although she wants to keep Cecilia within the bounds of propriety, fails because of her lack of energy and practical capability; likewise, Doña Rosa fails when she sends her son into public concubinage and indirectly to his death. As we see, Señora Mendizábal is repeated in these two women.

María del Rosario Alarcón (Charo), the "light brown" mother of

Cecilia, and a shadow dragged sinuously through the story, is the picture of insanity and as such becomes the most pathetic and acute concretization of what might be called the tragic destiny of the mulatto woman. She is the most direct and clear antecedent of the heroine's "fatality": Cecilia will be the picture of her (272), she will have a similar life cycle, and by apparently different routes mother and daughter will come together in the Paula Hospital (a women's jail) (547). Clearly a "woman of mixed races," Rosario will become "obsessed with the daughter's saying that since she had been born white, she disdained having a black mother" (292); thus, the root of her mental illness is in the ethnic values of the people of Cuba. Her madness reveals to us the dramatic tension that occurs in the psyche of the mulatto woman whose child almost belongs to the privileged race or is on the way to becoming a member of it.

This cycle of sex and sorrow, which has been the lot of the great-grandmother, the grandmother, and the mother, will be repeated in the protagonist, Cecilia Valdés, who is to all appearances white (448). "It wasn't forty days after her birth" that she was taken to the Royal House of Charity, because Don Cándido "could not and ought not give her his name" (61); and it was "necessary that the girl have a name, a name she wouldn't be ashamed of tomorrow or later, the name of Valdés with which she might make a good match" (60–61). In that charitable institution she stayed the necessary time for acquiring the surname established by the rules for the charges who lived there. There she would be nursed by María de la Regla, who according to Don Cándido's plans could not return her to her mother. When Rosario went mad, the grandmother took over the maternal functions. So Cecilia bore not only the biological marks of cross-breeding but, more important, the social stamp of the not quite legal union of her progenitors. This irregular status caused her to have a disorderly concept of her existence, a will to exploit life. When María Josefa died, the young girl would repeat the vicious circle of concubinage.

This erratic and licentious life is noticeable in the first formal appearance of the character, when the eleven-year-old girl gets the attention of everyone in the district of El Angel. Following a rather primitive narrative technique, Villaverde first presents a detailed account of her external appearance and then proceeds to a psychological characterization:

She was like the virgins of the great painters. For along with a high forehead crowned with copious, black, naturally wavy hair she had very regular features: a straight nose that projected between the eyebrows and being somewhat short, raised her lip slightly, so as to reveal two rows of small, white teeth. Her eyebrows formed an arc and made more shade over her full, black eyes, which were all motion and fire. She had a small mouth with full lips showing more voluptuousness than strength of character. Her full, round cheeks and a dimple in her chin made a beautiful whole, which to be perfect would have required only a less mischievous expression. [67]

Perhaps the length of the citation can be excused because it illustrates Villaverde's narrative technique so well. In fact, this portrait of Cecilia is a mosaic with all its pieces detailed. But there is more. With regard to the appearance of her face, the author departs, not from a possible description of the reality he perceives (the beauty of an adolescent mulatto girl), but from a mental image he has made of his subject. Cecilia Valdés, a lively, marriageable mulatto girl, takes on a type preconceived by the author, and so her mien becomes "that of the virgins of the great painters." If because of her malicious expression she doesn't attain absolute perfection, it is this same element that makes her the archetype of mulatto beauty being seen as a fusion of white beauty and mulatto malice.

But if the rest of this long physical description of Cecilia keeps adapting itself to the nineteenth-century ideal of feminine beauty, it will be necessary to emphasize more clearly the character's black lineage, which has slipped in in this malicious look in her eyes. This element is introduced almost surreptitiously, as if the author were afraid of uglifying the "pretty" picture he has made, because Villaverde perceives the African features as antiaesthetic elements:

the living incarnation, speaking in the sense in which painters understand this word, but upon first looking at her, one noticed it in the color of her face, which although still sanguineous, had a little too much hue of ochre to be transparent and clear. To which race did this girl belong after all? It is hard to tell. Nevertheless, a well-trained eye would not miss the fact that

her red lips had a black border or edge, and that the brightness
of her face ended in a kind of penumbra near where her hair
began. Her blood was not pure, and one could surely tell that
in the third or fourth generation back it was mixed with African
blood. [67–68]

Physically, Cecilia Valdés is the product of a juxtaposition of basic
African features with a concept of abstract Western feminine beauty,
the African features perceived as a detraction to the whole. The
cultural background of the author impedes his appreciation of black
beauty (contrary to the case of Anselmo Suárez y Romero) and his
ability to create an authentic quadroon. Cecilia Valdés is still beautiful, no matter if she is a mulatto. G. R. Coulthard is right when he
says that the portrait Villaverde makes of her "is almost of a white
woman, and her beauty bears a European stamp." [26]

In the characterization of Cecilia, some elements of her temperament have already been assessed—voluptuousness and malice; now
other "psychological" adjectives will be added with which to "flavor"
her personality. What is offered is simply an outline of behavior.
The girl comes through as happy and lively, and she always goes
around "more smiley than little bells" (68). With such a brief outline,
Villaverde commences to trot the protagonist around Christ's Square
in order to reveal her "moral makeup" and her conduct in her social
environment. She pilfers rolls, cracklings, fruit, and little things in
food stores (68); "she incites suspicions and fears," and she nurtures
"hopes of bastard lineage in the hearts of young men" (68). Flesh
for brothel and concubinage, "reared in the city streets" (69), the
jealous woman who later motivates the homicidal hand of José
Dolores Pimienta is presented to us here as a young pubescent girl.

Five or six years later, Cecilia has been transformed into a regal
young lady. With her intimate friend Nemesia, she makes a triumphal
entrance to the ball held to honor the saint's day of "the rich and
magnificient mulatto woman," Mercedes Ayala (85). Already Cecilia
is considered the "Venus of the hybrid Afro-Caucasian race," because
the only African feature she has is her "slightly bronze" color. The
young woman is the model of the white colonial woman: "There was
no one more beautiful nor more capable of upsetting the judgment
of a man in love . . . on account of the regularity of her features, the
symmetry of her form, the narrowness of her waist in contrast with

the breadth of her shoulders, her amorous expression, and the slightly bronze color of her skin" (88–89).

The near whiteness of the protagonist is continually emphasized by pointing out the similarity between her and Adela, Leonardo de Gamboa's younger sister. The similarity between the half-sisters is so great that even Isabel de Ilincheta confuses the Valdés girl with her future sister-in-law: "Cecilia without her disguise—for her mask had fallen to her shoulders, her black hair flowing, held back only at the level of her forehead by a red ribbon, with her cheeks flushed and her eyes sparkling with anger—was the image of Leonardo de Gamboa's younger sister" (287). The young Gamboa also was to notice this resemblance between his sister and his beloved (347); and so did the black nurse, María de la Regla (492). After all, Cecilia's beauty is of a "European type," which her own grandmother knows very well: "Although it's wrong for me to say it, she is truly the most beautiful woman ever seen in the world. Nobody would say she has even a bit of color. She looks like a white woman. Her beauty makes me crazy and beside myself" (291).

Morúa Delgado has pointed to a contradiction between the physical appearance of the character described here and the nickname given Cecilia in the novel, "the little bronze virgin." [27] In my opinion, this appellation is one more element that emphasizes Cecilia's beauty, for it is the same one given to the patron saint of Cuba, Nuestra Señora de la Caridad del Cobre (Our Lady of Charity of Bronze.) But if to the blacks Cecilia is white (327), the heroine nevertheless has inside her the whole complex of contradictions of the mulatto. The "coarse gallantry" with which the men treat her "because of the fact that she was of the hybrid and inferior race" (96) causes the girl to react with "pride and vanity, the secret roots of her imperious nature" (96). And so, when an acute consciousness of her mixed blood strikes her, along with it comes the traditional aspiration of the mulatto woman—to be joined with a white man: "Without shame or hesitation, she continually showed her preference for men of the superior white race, as if from them she could expect social distinction and possessions" (96).

Thus, a relationship with a white man means rising in the social and economic scale of the colony; but it also implies the desire to "better the race," that is, to erase the "Negro stigma" from her descendants. Because mulattoes cannot identify with either of the two races, alienation becomes part of their psychology, along with a state of conflict and a sense of insecurity. But Villaverde didn't capture this fundamental psychic trait; he simply sensed it, and he expressed it incompletely. The girl acts out of mulatto pride, jealousy, or vengeance, but there is no deep analysis of these motives, which seem to be just social reactions, not something rooted in the very depths of her being—hence, the melodramatic or simply conventional tendency that directs her behavior throughout the story. As Manuel de la Cruz has correctly said, Cecilia Valdés "does not have all the definition her character calls for." [28]

With the same superficial and external vision with which he has characterized the protagonist, Villaverde brings in quite a collection of black people, most of whom remain simply *costumbrista* portraits. However, it is worthwhile to single out some of the characters, either because of the relative importance they have in linking the motives of the action or because of their ideological, historical, or typical significance.

Nemesia, the heroine's intimate friend, follows the local characterization of the mulatto woman: beautiful, "free," but without the tragic dimension it had in Cecilia. Nemesia has had the same "street" rearing as Cecilia (78), and she moves in the same environment; but unlike the quadroon, she cannot aspire to the hand of a white man, because, as the daughter of a black, she is, according to María Josefa, "a ragged little brown girl, with strong color" (78). To this ethnic inferiority one must add the aesthetic: the beauty of Nemesia cannot be compared with Cecilia's (89). This double inferiority causes in Nemesia a feeling of envy that will seek in intrigue an escape valve and a means to triumph over the social condition in which she finds herself.

This psychological and moral makeup is manifest in the perverse behavior Nemesia adopts with relation to José Dolores Pimienta, Cecilia, and Leonardo de Gamboa and their amorous triangle. She wants to manipulate them so as to achieve her own ends—the love of the white youth, or at least his break with Cecilia. Thus, more than once she succeeds in inciting anger, displeasure, jealousy, and rage against Leonardo in Cecilia by telling her about his relationships with white girls, especially with Isabel de Ilincheta. At other times, acting as an intermediary in behalf of José Dolores, she is working to her own advantage: "He is very susceptible to love, and he likes brown girls. It isn't so difficult as it seems. Let's see whether I can kill two birds with one stone. She for José Dolores, and he for me. It can be done, it can be" (212–13).

The brother of this little intriguer, José Dolores Pimienta, is a musician by vocation and talent, although he is a tailor by necessity. "A young mulatto, well built, and with not a bad face" (84), he expresses through music "the strength of his passion for Cecilia" (89). Faithful to the point of blind obediencce, "very pleasant, courteous, and attentive," he has succeeded, in spite of these qualities, in obtaining from the young girl only one or two signs of favor "among the men of his class" (97). His look—distracted, sad, and gloomy—reveals a romantic temperament that "agonizes with love and jealousy" for the one he will never possess (100). On the occasions when Cecilia is indisputably the queen of the parties, his restlessness and passion find their "outlet on the keys of the clarinet," adding charm and liveliness to the fiesta (101). His is an unspoken, silent, suffering love. As Nemesia says to Cecilia: "He obviously loves you, adores, you, idolizes you, sighs for you; but he is so timid that he will not dare tell you what black eyes you have, much less imagine you are coming after him" (320).

This idealization of the love feelings of the mulatto is a faithful representation of the personality Villaverde gives him. He is an absolutely fictitious and conventionalized being; moreover, we have the constant impression that José Dolores is a recourse the author uses whenever he needs it. Indeed, his appearance in the story is governed by a prior and gratuitous function decreed for him, as can be shown very clearly in the denouement of the novel (546). Just like Nemesia and even Cecilia at times, this character appears and disappears without maintaining an authentic identity—an identity that is really nonexistent in any case, because Villaverde did not know how to create an authentic literary character.

As mentioned above, many black characters animate the pages of Cecilia Valdés. It is not the object of the present work to make a detailed study of each of these, but it is appropriate to emphasize the attitude Villaverde assumes in trying to depict them. Among those drawn in genre style are Dolores Santa Cruz, the black woman impoverished by the plundering of a white and driven mad because of it; Aponte and Pío, the slave calash drivers of the Gamboa family; Dionisio, the cook in the same house; and "Malanga," whose description provides a magnificient illustration of how Villaverde observes and paints such characters: "The third passer-by, likewise a black man, was a type 'sui generis,' set off both by his costume and by his actions and appearance. His outfit was made up of bell trousers, with embroidery, very wide over part of the leg, narrow around the ankle; and a white shirt with a wide collar, with dog-tooth embroidery instead of a border" (456). And the author proceeds to describe in all its tedious detail Malanga's handkerchief, shoes, hat, hairdo, and even the gold rings hanging from the tawdry black man's ears.

This is always the pattern. The emphasis is always on the appearance, the local color, and the point of view of an illustrator—in the true sense of that word—which is the point of view Villaverde takes. What attracts his attention, and what he thinks is important about these characters, is the type; and that is what makes them worthy of a place in the novel. It is not the man who is of prime interest here; it is the stamp of his outside appearance. As a result we have a superficial, elemental, and primitive depiction of the black man.

We can find other social manifestations of the Cuban slave system in the story, but these elements do not go beyond the historico-documentary. At times the novel becomes a chronicle. The heroine might have been the unifying and purging element in this motley conglomeration of episodes, but because she is just a sketch, often eclipsed by other characters, she is reduced to one more color motif in this disparate story. As Enrique Anderson-Imbert said, "the novel of the mulatto woman Cecilia Valdés has fallen short; unsuccessful as art, what is interesting to the reader is the raw reality, not really fashioned into a novel." [29]

III   Gertrudis Gómez de Avellaneda: *Sab*

The basic purpose of the narrators we have studied thus far was to portray the slave society of Cuba; it is for this reason that their characters sometimes are obscured by the vast panorama they are trying to describe. The social aspects are what interests them essentially, and the personal element is subordinated to that interest. An intense sentimental note can be present, as in *Francisco,* but it is the picture of slavery that predominates in the story and on which the being and existence of these fictional creatures ultimately depend. In *Sab,* on the contrary, the vision of society is the accessory and is used only to the extent and in the manner necessary to emphasize the tragic nature of the hero. To be a romantic character, Sab has to be a slave and a mulatto: if he were not a slave with dark skin, he would be reduced to a sensitive and passionate person who attains happiness in his possibly requited love. His tragic destiny would escape him. Francisco, by contrast, is a black slave to whom Suárez y Romero has added the trappings of romantic idealization to make his character more pathetic, at the same time rendering his oppressors more hateful and contemptible. Without these adornments of the romantic period, Francisco's destiny would still be as terrible—or, better, more authentically terrible. Finally, Sab follows the vision of a tropical scene re-created from Europe and seen through eyes veiled by the gauze of the romantic escapist dream.

Gertrudis Gómez de Avellaneda (1814–73), author of an extensive body of lyricodramatic works and prose works in various forms, began her work in narrative fiction with her novel Sab. Although it was published in Madrid in 1841, the composition of this story of hopeless love between a mulatto slave and his white mistress goes back to the nostalgic period following the author's departure from Cuba in 1836. It is the only extensive narrative she wrote with a Cuban theme, and this and Guatimozín (1846) are the only works of this type in which she takes up a Spanish-American subject.

According to an autobiography she wrote in 1850, she started writing Sab to distract herself when she was in Bordeaux, newly arrived from Cuba,[30] but in a letter to Don Antonio Neira, dated 28 February 1843, she stated that "in periods of idleness, I was writing desultorily on Sab, which I began in Lisbon in 1838 and which I finished in Seville in 1839." [31] This last datum is corroborated in her first account of her life, in which she does not mention starting to write Sab while she was in France.[32] In addition, the prologue to the first edition states that "this little novel slept for three years in the bottom of her paper-case." [33] It is most likely that the nostalgic memories of her native island and the impressive picture of slavery added to her own life experience—her feminist ideas in constant conflict with her conservative, peninsular family heritage—were the creative impulse behind this novel. As we shall see, Avellaneda identifies the situation of women with that of the slave; when she began a more independent life around 1838, the form of Sab started to gel and to acquire contours.

Indeed, on 28 September 1839, Avellaneda wrote to Ignacio de Cepeda y Alcalde that she had sent the first ten chapters of the novel for a reading to an unnamed compatriot, "a man of education and taste," whose criticism encouraged her to continue the story.[34] According to the anonymous Cuban, "the descriptive part is drawn with exactitude and variety and the characters are well delineated, and vigorously developed." By April of 1840, the novel must have been completed, because on 29 April she wrote to Cepeda telling him that a subscription had been started in Seville, Granada, and Málaga to defray the editorial expenses.[35] But the novel was not published in Seville; it appeared in Madrid the next year, dedicated to Don Alberto Lista. From his retirement in Cádiz, Lista thanked the author for the dedication with a letter full of praise. According to him, the merit of the novel "consists in having succeeded in drawing the reader's sympathy to the unrequited lovers." [36]

During that period, Avellaneda was an avid reader of Rousseau; of Millevoye, "almost as sweet a poet as Lamartine"; of Lamartine himself, conceived of as "deeper than Millevoye"; of Walter Scott, "the first prose writer of Europe and the most distinguished novelist of the period"; of Madame de Staël; "of the immortal and divine Chateaubriand," whose *Atala* filled her with romantic enthusiasm because of its "scenes of nature and its primitive souls"; of Lista, Quintana, and Heredia; and curiously, of Montesquieu, whose complete works she took with her on a visit to the castle of Bredas in the vicinity of Bordeaux. She was an indefatigable reader, a fact that caused a certain amount of ironic mockery from the Galician family: they called her the "doctor" and "atheist." [37]

Sab grew out of Avellaneda's reading and the experiences she had had in Cuba, and also out of her independent nature, which never became reconciled to the conventional patterns society set up for a woman. Avellaneda felt like a prisoner, and for this reason she identified with the slave. The psychological basis of the novel is this compassion for the slave, with whom she shares the painful sense of being deprived of liberty: "Oh, women! Poor, blind victims! Like slaves they drag their chains patiently and lower their head under the yoke of human laws" (2: 143).

Later, she attacks the institution of marriage, the great torment of her existence: "With no other guide than their ignorant and credulous heart, they choose a master for life. The slave can at least change masters, or he can hope that by saving money he can buy his freedom some day: but a woman, when she raises her weakened hands and her offended brow, hears the monstrous, sepulchral voice that cries to her: 'In your tomb' " (2:143). The situation of a married woman, to Avellaneda, is worse than that of a poor slave. It is strange that a work so impregnated with feminism as Helena Percas Ponseti's has taken no note of this element.[38] The feminist element and the liberal ideology that nourished Avellaneda during this period are the source of the decided abolitionism that permeates the novel.

Sab has been denied classification as an antislavery story with a myopia bordering on blindness. Pastor Díaz, a great friend of the author, affirmed that the hero "could have been drawn in some other status and in some other society, and perhaps at least for us, he could have been more interesting if he had more verisimilitude." [39] Emilio Cotarelo y Mori also comments that "there is no antislavery protest here"; Sab "could, for example, have been a Spanish commoner in love with a stylish lady, as in so many romantic novels and stories." Helena Percas Ponseti, refuting this judgment, thinks that "the antislavery message of the work is absolutely clear." [40] Precisely because it was abolitionist, the novel was not allowed entry into Cuba, as shown in the Havana National Archives; and the author left it out of the edition she prepared for her *Obras literarias* (1869–71) in order to avoid censorship on the island and thus to secure the very important Cuban market.

As early as the prologue, we come upon Avellaneda's confession of radicalism with regard to slavery during the period when she was writing the novel. Later, Sab describes the slave's workday in all its abjection:

> under that fiery sky the slave, almost nude, works all morning without rest, and at the terrible noon, panting, overwhelmed by the weight of the firewood or cane he carries on his back, burned by the rays of the sun that toasts his skin, he can finally enjoy all the pleasure life holds for him: two hours of sleep and a small ration. When the evening comes to console the braised earth with its breezes and its shade, and all nature rests, the slave goes to water with his sweat and tears the sugar caldrons where the night has no shade and the breeze no freshness: for there the wood fire has replaced the fire of the sun. [1:15–16]

Then, in the interviews with Teresa, he expresses again the misery of having been born a slave, here in a Rousseauistic tone:

> But oh! They deny to the Negro what they allow to wild animals, which they consider equal to him: they let the animals live in the woodlands where they were born, but they tear the Negro away from his. A debased slave, he will bequeath slavery and debasement to his children by inheritance, and these miserable children will ask in vain for the sylvan life of their forefathers. In further torment, they will be condemned to see men like themselves, for whom fortune and ambition open a thousand roads to glory and power; while they cannot have ambition, nor can they hope for any future. [2: 40]

Finally, the protagonist, by means of rhetorical questions, emphasizes the essential equality of all men without distinction of race or color: "The great chief of this great human family, can he have made different laws for those born with black skin or white skin? Have they not the same needs; can one group have the right to enslave, and the others the obligation to obey?" (2: 131–32).

The ideological liberalism of the period in which the novel was written is also expressed in two other topics characteristic of Hispanic-American literature of that time: anti-Spanish views, and the exaltation and idealization of the Indian. The former, as we shall see later in the story *Guatimozín*, is historical; but already in *Sab* the conquest and colonization of America are described in the most somber colors. In a sentimental rapture, Carlota exclaims: "I've never been able to read tranquilly the bloody history of the conquest of America. My God! What a lot of horrors! My, it seems incredible to me that men can come to such extremes of barbarity" (1: 136). The Indian is categorized as an innocent victim whose paradise has been destroyed by the historic process of colonization. This retrospective utopia has the effect of an implicit criticism of contemporary society: "Here those children of nature lived happy and innocent: this virgin land did not need to be watered with the sweat of slaves to produce for them: everywhere it offered them shade and fruits, water and flowers" (1: 137).

We have seen how negroism and Indianism are integrated in this sentimental argumentation that has its roots in Rousseau and Chateaubriand. But there is also another kind of integration of these themes that is concerned with future history. As she shows the constant anxiety of the Cuban colonials over the slave uprising on the island of Santo Domingo (it was because of this that the author's family left Cuba), Avellaneda sees in the possible slave rebellion a revenge for the Indian: "The land that was once showered with blood will be showered again: the descendants of the oppressors will be oppressed, and the black men will be the terrible avengers of the copper men" (1: 135).

These thematic coordinates, in addition to the sentimental idealism (coming from Rousseau but learned in Chateaubriand) that informs Avellaneda's thought, are the determining features in the creation of the central character of the novel. Thus, the black is the product of two prior images that act upon the author, one intellectual and the other aesthetic. Sab is a double myth, important to dissect, not only in order to point out the components of this figure but also to discover the attitude from which the author departs. These are keys in our efforts to understand how well Avellaneda has grasped and expressed the character of the black protagonist.

Helena Percas Ponseti has said that "what stands out in this novel is its psychological richness, presented simply and without subtleties in the style." Earlier, referring to the central character, she had commented, "it is an abstraction; but at the same time it is a flesh and blood character." [41] For his part, Aurelio Mitjans had pointed out the "obvious improbability in the love of the outcast" [42] and with regard to the evident conventionalism of the whole story, diminished by the author's direct observation, José Antonio Portuondo and Lorenzo García Vega are in agreement. Referring to the treatment of the landscape in the novel, Portuondo wrote that "the depiction of the tropics, so much enjoyed by the romantic writers, especially the French, turns out less false (in her novel) because of the persistence of childhood memories." García Vega has pointed out the theatrical quality in Sab—"of curtains and flies"—transforming nature in Cuba.[43] The elements that have attracted critical attention most consistently—the protagonist and the landscape—seem to be endowed with a double value, as shown by the scholars we have cited: the value derived from the author's retrospective but direct view, and that which stems from the romantic period in which Avellaneda lived.

If by "psychological richness" we mean the scholarly understanding and management of a plan of abstract characterization, which in this case bears the stamp of romanticism, then Sab would be a psychologically rich character; but he would also be essentially false. This lack of focus in the conception of the protagonist, a product, as we have seen, of basically bookish coordinates, is the basis of the improbability mentioned by Mitjans. The author's intent—to show that the black is equal to or superior to the white—is praiseworthy; but in trying to prove it, her deep-rooted romanticism causes her to conceive a conventional black figure, the fruit of her reading in the French romanticists. The result is that Sab, a black by dint of certain very weak epidermal features and the tone of exoticism that goes with these features, is a symbiosis of what we might call the "noble Negro" and the romantic hero. Let us consider how this character follows both characterological schemes.

In Spanish peninsular literature, the idealization of the black appears in Lope de Rueda. As Raymond Sayers has shown, the character Eulalia in *Eufemia* "is a new conception: the romantic Negro girl." [44] In Lope de Vega, the concept of the noble Negro does not differ greatly from the idealization of the Moor, as can be seen in the *Santo Negro Rosambuco de la ciudad de Palermo*. But it is in the work of the English writer Aphra Behen (1640–89) that the image of the noble Negro first appears as the romantics will conceive it. In her story *Oroonoka* (1688), the black character is presented as a "gallant warrior, a high-minded prince, an excellent conversationalist, a modest lover." Sayers's remark that "if no such legend sprang up in Brazil, it is probably because the Negro slave was too common a figure to permit of spontaneous romanticizing" [45] is valid also for the treatment of this theme in Cuba. Exceptions are Suárez y Romero and especially Avellaneda, who because of her separation from the blacks in both space and time was inclined to present a much more idealized picture of them than that offered by Tanco or Villaverde.

Sab, with "an air so uncommon to his class" (1: 18), is an exceptional being—almost unique. A mulatto, born of an African black woman and a white gentleman, a doubly aristocratic blood runs in his veins, for his mother "was born free and a princess in a country where her color was not a sign of slavery" (1: 20). When this woman, a brief synthesis of the romantic heroine, arrived in the New World, "the poor unhappy girl grieved disconsolate for two years, unable to resign herself to the horrible change in her fate, until an absolute passion [love] blazed with full force in that African heart" (1: 21). But we would deceive ourselves if we supposed that Sab's values were African values, as the pride he expresses in his maternal ancestry might seem to indicate. On the contrary, the mulatto's point of view is the point of view of a white, for he immediately adds, *"in spite of her color,* my mother was beautiful" (1: 21) The italics, which are ours, show clearly the white point of view that Avellaneda attributes to this slave.

This color prejudice can be seen also in the physical description of Sab. "He was tall, and of regular proportions, and his face was a strange combination in which the crossing of two races could be noted, without his being a perfect mulatto" (1: 11). In fact, the only basic negroid feature, or what is thought of as negroid in Cuba, is "thick, purplish lips, elements that indicated his African origin" (1: 12). His skin color is a "yellowish white"; his hair, "black and shiny like the wings of a crow, falls in locks not in kinks"; and his chin is "prominent and triangular" (1: 11–12). Although Sab wears rustic clothing, because of his features and his bearing Enrique Otway takes him for a rich *hacendado,* "one of the distinguished landowners from around here, who when they are at their country haciendas like to dress like simple farmhands" (1: 17). Thus, the external picture Avellaneda gives us of Sab is of a well-heeled colonial, a member of the Cuban agricultural aristocracy.

The external picture of the man is of one of those "faces that are noticed immediately and which once seen are never forgotten" (1: 12), and thus Sab acquires the romantic "pose" by which his movements are regulated. A good proof of this is the first chapter of the first part, where the mulatto's personality is presented all at once. Sab, as he speaks of the blacks' suffering, brings to his lips "a melancholy smile" (1: 16); his bearing "seemed to reveal something grand and noble that drew one's attention" (1: 17); again, his smile, "more and more melancholy, took on a certain appearance of disdain" (1: 19); his voice shows lively emotion when he remembers his childish escapades with Carlota (1: 22); and when he recognizes the Englishman, "one can sense an incomprehensible upheaval inside him, revealed by the vertical wrinkles that covered his face and a sinister light" in his eyes, "like a flash of lightning that shines among dark clouds." Finally, "he fixed his eyes on the sky, heaved a deep sigh, and fell on a bank" (1: 26). As we see, the character is conceived

in the romantic pose that predetermines his actions which develop in
an ever-heightened dramatic progression as we approach the catastrophic end of the narrative. For example, when he faces the storm
with Enrique and it occurs to him that he could kill Enrique at that
point, the mulatto's look becomes obsessive, like that of a crazy man
(1: 71–72).

This set of stock gestures and attitudes is the copy of a romantic
soul that in the correct and figurative sense of the word is white.
The nobility of his spirit, which is revealed when he first appears,
impresses Carlota's future husband so quickly that in his first encounter with her he comments on this quality (1: 58). Then, on the
trip to the Cubitas Mountains, the Indian Martina echoes what everyone feels; after they have mentioned the small boy's rescue by the
slave, the old woman exclaims, "the soul of that poor Sab is beautiful,
very beautiful" (1: 161). But it is Teresa who really comprehends the
"whiteness" of that extraordinary being. To all outward appearances
apathetic but in fact deeply sensitive, it is she who understands what
a sacrifice the slave has made in twice saving the life of his rival.
This is why Sab says to her in his delirium: "You have penetrated
this heart, you know all its secrets, you know how much I detest this
life that I've saved twice, and you understand the whole price of my
generosity" (1: 171–72).

In the love conflict that the four central characters of the novel
create, the antithetic parallelism Avellaneda establishes between Sab
and Enrique becomes apparent. By contraposing the mulatto and the
Englishman, the author clearly discloses the white soul enclosed in
the mulatto body, which is the slave's ultimate being. By way of
contrast, Avellaneda describes the Englishman as a man attracted by
riches and "too much indoctrinated in the mercantile and speculative
spirit of his father" (1: 44). Indeed, although in love with Carlota, he
marries her as a means of building his capital, and he would give up
the young woman's hand if she were not possessed of a solid fortune.
But, even worse, Avellaneda draws him as a mean spirit, incapable
of feeling the great passion of love; hence, he is the antithesis of
the romantic hero and consequently of Sab. The spiritual mediocrity
of the young Englishman shows itself at the moment when Carlota
realizes that her fiancé is not an exceptional spirit (1: 68).

Enrique himself also realizes this when he senses the love Sab
feels for Carlota. Moreover, "perhaps the secret voice of his con-

science told him at that moment that if he exchanged his heart for the heart of that poor unhappy being, he would be more worthy of the young woman's enthusiastic love" (1: 114). Sab, for his part, notices the ironic conflict that has arisen between him and Enrique, "a hundred times more unworthy than I, in spite of his snowy white skin and his golden hair" (2: 28). At the same time, he is very much aware of the pain of being a mulatto: if he were not one, he could aspire to the love of his "señorita." His feelings come out in the sentimental talk he has with his horse: "he who put me onto this earth of misery and pain," Sab says, "should have given the mulatto the body of the white man, and the white man the soul of the mulatto" (1: 95), so that body and spirit would have been in harmony.

This conflict between a black ethnos and a white ego dramatically accentuates the romantic character of the protagonist. In Sab, we have the characteristic features of the romantic hero along with the dramatic and exotic emphasis of blackness. Consequently, the force that dominates the personality of the hero is of course the exaltation of sensibility and of the passion of love. Sab's extreme suffering reaches its climax exactly when the marriage of Carlota and Enrique becomes inevitable, at the same time that the slave realizes that "his mission on earth is accomplished" (2: 73). Again, the only creature who can be the object of his sentimental effusions is the beautiful horse he owns: it is to this animal that the mulatto directs his lamentation, and thus we understand the state of hopeless turmoil the slave now expresses freely. In the paroxysm of his suffering, he exclaims: "Heaven will be his in this life, and hell will be mine: because hell is here, in my heart and my head" (2: 72).

By means of extreme romantic exaltation of his passion, Sab comes to understand the spiritual freedom of his own soul, in spite of his slave status. And it is curious that this is revealed to him through his filial relationship with Martina, which at the moment of death throws a new, bold light on his feelings. At this moment, recalling his life, Sab has learned to distinguish clearly between physical and moral liberty: "the chains that imprison the hands need not oppress the soul" (2: 124). The spirit must remain free, and the measure of this liberty is a man's "moral grandeur" and also the romantic passion that possesses him. Thus, the romantic view of life, embodied in a slave, is given a new tragic expression when with physical and social fetters it accentuates the basic restlessness and tragic destiny of a person who is nevertheless morally free and able to play the heroic role required by the romantic epoch.

Because he has "chains on his hands," this epochal requirement will take in Sab the forms specific to his servile state. And so we find a heroism appropriate to a servant, as is apparent in the relationship between Sab and his rival Enrique. At the moment when the servant could have overcome Enrique, the memory of Carlota and especially the knowledge that his soul is capable of being "great and virtuous" detain him. "Here I have him at my feet, unable to speak and unconscious, this man I hate. One stroke of the will would reduce him to nothing, and that will is mine . . . mine, a poor slave whom he does not suspect of having a soul superior to his own . . . able to love . . . able to hate" (1: 74). For this moment, the slave is physically free, but the important points are the consciousness he has of his liberty and the contradiction between his social condition and his own being. Sab "serves" in this concrete instance, not because of a physical obligation, but because of his own moral imperative and the memory of the woman he loves. Thus, he has risen to a new essential liberty and, naturally, to the peak of romantic idealization. This element of "essential" liberty can also be appreciated in the decision he makes: to give Carlota a prize lottery ticket so that Enrique will marry her, at a time when her fortune has diminished a great deal (2: 125). By this act, Sab becomes the black man with a "white" soul and, at the same time, the free slave. These fundamentally romantic contradictions are the pillars on which the protagonist's romantic nature rests. Blackness and slavery are the means of sharpening the basic features of Sab's romantic personality. Avellaneda has created this character by making use of the requirements of the times, which for greater dramatic effect she has attributed to a black slave.

Where this essentially literary view can be seen most clearly is in the love relationship of the mulatto and his mistress, and especially in the gratuitousness of his love. Sab cannot hope to get anything out of the passion he nurtures for Carlota, except for the enjoyment of the sentiment that is devouring him. The young woman is "an object of veneration and tenderness" (1: 114) for the hero, and he knows that the girl can see nothing more in him than "her childhood companion and her first friend" (1: 124). Thus, although occasionally there is some slight physical contact—"a kiss on the hand like a red-hot coal" caused by a moment of "compassion" on Carlota's part

(1: 80)—the only way Sab can satisfy his passion is to carry it back to the infantile level: the obsessing image of Carlota as a child hanging ingenuously on his adolescent neck (1: 126). This is a love that has its basis in innocent childhood, a love that cannot be "stained" by the least liberty and that in the case of Sab achieves the consecration of a virgin death. The slave dies consumed by this utterly pure love: "I die without having spotted my life: I die burned in the sacred fire of love" (2: 139).

Here again, the specific circumstances of the character underline the basic romanticism of such a love. Allowing for the fact that any physical consummation is impossible and taking advantage of the moral liberty he enjoys, Sab has decided to become the "spiritual slave" of his mistress. Thus, the slave who because of his awareness of his passionate being was free in the tribunal of his conscience, because of the deep exacerbation of the most characteristic element of his nature—impossible love—has again become a slave but, this time, a slave to love. And in this strange play of romantic contradictions, slavery, as a social institution, becomes the only possible means of maintaining such a relationship and even of propitiating it. This is clearly sensed by Enrique Otway, and our hero himself affirms it explicitly: "From my childhood I was bound to Carlota: I am her slave and I want to live and die in her service" (1: 23–24).

Within the internal logic of the novel, Teresa, as she dies, can say to Carlota in all justice: "You have possessed, without coming to know it, one of those great, ardent souls, born for sublime sacrifices, one of those exceptional souls that pass over the earth like a breath of God" (2: 123–24).

Sab is thus the incarnation of a literary myth, an absolutely false and conventional being, an apparently unique species, but basically topical and generic.

IV   Francisco Calcagno: *Romualdo*

In the work of Francisco Calcagno (1827–1903), named earlier as a member of the second generation of Cuban romantics, we can see that the abolitionist novel undergoes a slight change of direction. If it is indeed true that because of the arrangement of the movement of the plot *Romualdo: Uno de tantos* (1869) gives us the impression of a pseudorealistic feuilleton, it is no less true that in the very sketchy characterization of the protagonist in this short novel we can sense a greater effort to adapt the figure to the real image of a mulatto slave. Romualdo constitutes a rectification of Francisco and obviously of Sab, but still without substantially differentiating ethnic features.

The indefatigable Calcagno devoted his life to teaching, historical research, and the abolitionist idea, besides writing numerous novels. Examples of this work are his *Diccionario biográfico cubano* (New York, 1878), still a basic reference, the first attempted in Cuba, and a very useful work; the little book *Poetas de color;* and a series of historical and scientific narratives in the style of Jules Verne.[46]

With *Romualdo,* which the author himself called an abolitionist novel, Calcagno began his work in the narrative genre. Although it was published in 1891, the novel was written in 1869, as clearly acknowledged by the author.[47] It is the narration of a case of *plagium,* a term used in Cuba, as in ancient Rome, to designate the kidnapping of a free man in order to make him a slave. This phenomenon was not unusual: Calcagno himself offers abundant examples in the course of his story (85). What gives this novel the melodramatic tone we have mentioned is not the substance of his plot but the events that revolve around the central point.

In fact, the plot is built on a series of chance occurrences. Romualdo is sold to his own father, who is ignorant of his new slave's origin; Clemencia, the concubine of Don Jacobo, Romualdo's abductor, is also the niece of Felicia, the mother of the unhappy Romualdo; the priest of Magarabomba discovers all this by means of grotesque evidence, and when justice is about to be done, the hero, who had fled to the forest, is killed by a gang of *ranchadores* (men who round up runaways). All these episodes develop dizzily, leaving the reader in a state of confusion and astonishment.

But in the narrative—literarily very inferior to others examined in this chapter—the accent of extreme sensibility attributed to the slave has diminished a great deal, leaving him in an antiheroic state. "He was of no use as a hero; he was indifferent to everything: he was a machine that limited its action to following movement initiated by others" (141). And Romualdo is not an exceptional being like Francisco the martyr or Sab the tormented; his reaction is one of hate in the face of oppression by the white man, and he opts for joining a colony of runaways who plan to rebel against the unjust system that oppresses him. Thus it is that he "found himself in the situation of hating everything" (107). He appears for the first time in the story as a cimarron:

> tall, robust, with a sullen frown, bronze skin: he is a mulatto. His look is melancholy and a little savage, his drawn-in mouth seems to breathe hatred, his bare feet are riddled with brambles: one would say he's the gloomy spirit of the woods. His build is athletic, but his whole body shows the depression caused by hunger and privation: he is not afraid of solitude or rough weather, but the barking of a dog in the distance startles him. [17]

Romualdo is indeed "one of many." There is nothing exceptional about his relationship with Dorotea: they are "just slave-type loves, without permission from the priest or anybody" (21). The black woman, who "had died no one knew when, because nobody remembers when a slave died" (21), has given him a daughter, Blassa, whom the slave loves "the way Negroes love, perhaps more savagely, but more than the whites" (24). Even the protagonist is pictured as already worn out from the work in the sugar mill: at forty, he is "bent over by suffering and work and appears to be sixty" (26). Compared, for example, to Francisco, the prototype of masculine black beauty, Romualdo lacks the natural gifts that might make him physically attractive: "he must have been ugly . . . with a drawn-in forehead, big lips, a prominent jaw, and a ferocious look" (19).

But the image Calcagno gives us of the black slave, although it is accurate in its isolated details, is also more superficial, incomplete, and ingenuous than those by Suárez y Romero, Villaverde, or Avellaneda. When we read this text, we come to the conclusion that the learned professor was not a novelist. In the last analysis, he is writing history that he hopes will also be illustrative of a phenomenon in Cuban society. More than anything else, the novel is a document for a historian, who can even find copies of sale contracts for slaves in its pages. Moreover, there is no effort to make a psychological study of the other characters: they are impelled to act only by the arbitrary and casuistic arrangement of the events narrated. For this reason, whereas we place Tanco, Suárez, and Villaverde with Balzac and Avellaneda with Chateaubriand, we must place Francisco Calcagno among the many Spanish-American disciples of the feuilletonist Eugène Sue.

Chapter Five

The End of the Century: Realism, Naturalism, and Artistic Prose

In this chapter, we shall undertake to examine the characterization of the black protagonist in the Cuban novel of the last quarter of the nineteenth century. In that part of the century, Raimundo Lazo distinguishes two generations in Cuba: the generations of José Martí (1853–95) and Julián del Casal (1863–93).[1] Both correspond, however, to the group that brought the romantic movement to a close in Spanish America and initiated the transition to modernism, according to the generational groupings established by José Juan Arrom.[2] The differentiation made by Lazo is justified only by the greater and more "generalized adherence to the renovative impulses of modernism" that is seen in the second of the two groups;[3] we should bear in mind, however, that "the attainment of political liberty and the desire to make the same dream of national integration a reality" make them "intimately related" and give them "the same polemic and oratorical character."[4] Besides, as far as our area of investigation is concerned, a man from the first group, Martí Morúa Delgado, is the most modern in the strict sense of the term, for he introduces the narrative techniques of the naturalist school. For these reasons, we prefer to include Antonio Zambrana and Ramón Meza in this chapter along with Morúa, but we distinguish them from Morúa in their technique and in their conception of the novel. In this section we shall take up, first, the realistic view of the black in the work of Zambrana and Meza and, subsequently, the naturalist interpretation of Morúa Delgado.

I Antonio Zambrana: *El negro Francisco*

El negro Francisco (1875) by Antonio Zambrana y Vázquez (1846–1922) is the last of the Cuban abolitionist novels. Because it was written in Chile where the author, a distinguished orator and political separatist, was making propaganda for Cuban independence, it was possible to publish it the same year it was finished. The novel is a reelaboration of the story with the same title written by Anselmo Suárez y Romero thirty years before, and Zambrana himself acknowledged his indebtedness to the romantic novelist. As he tells us in the introduction, when barely more than a child he had attended the literary *tertulias* held in the home of his uncle Ramón. At one of these sessions, one of the most important members of the literary group, Anselmo Suárez, was presented "with some sheets of paper in his hand, and after having assured his audience that they contained a story as sad as it was true, he began a reading that lasted more than two hours." [5] Suárez's story was a revelation to young Zambrana, who made an "irrevocable inner resolution not to be an accomplice of the slave system" (5–6). Later, some friends asked him to write a novel for Chile with a Cuban subject, and because slavery was the most characteristic aspect of Cuban society, his story necessarily had to revolve around that institution (6). Although "he who was then a boy cannot now have enough confidence in his boyish discernment to appreciate the artistic value of the story," he decided to use Suárez's theme "because no force of his imagination has succeeded in overcoming the memory his mind holds of the story just referred to" (6).

Zambrana's intention was to record the bare facts without any rhetorical or ideological additions: "slavery is a fact such that, after presenting it in its nakedness, any discourse one might make about it is a banality, and even the most insignificant reflection one might add to it can be considered an outrage to the reader's moral sense. So it was a question of recounting a fact, nothing more" (9). The desire for realism we see in these lines stems from the author's inner conviction that "nature always has a certain prestige over art, and there is in the truth something that the most exquisite and well-contrived invention cannot mimic" (6). This is why he decided to reuse Suárez's theme; he perceived it as an episode that had really occurred; that is, a true historical event—the truth that fantasy cannot surpass.

The essential thematic element that shapes the narration is Antonio Zambrana's militant abolitionism. In this man who was in Chile as an agent of the revolution of 1868, we do not perceive the anti-Spanish tone, just as we had not noticed it in the antislavery novel of romanticism. Moreover, Zambrana advances one step further in this line of thought when he proclaims that abolition of slavery must be the first concern of the Cuban, even taking precedence over the struggles for independence:

> Let them not concern themselves so much with combatting Spanish domination, with getting this or the other form of government, this or the other freedom, this or the other guarantee. Let them concern themselves above all for the Negroes. Instead of worrying about being exploited, let them worry about not exploiting. The enslavement suffered is terrible, but still more tremendous is that which is imposed. You say, oh, if the Cubans only were not slaves! I say, oh, if the Cubans did not *have* slaves! [165] [6]

Because of his strong feelings, the whole text is pervaded with a militant and authentic abolitionism that has very clearly penetrated the Cuban problem of that period: the island must perforce remain united to Spain as long as the crime of slavery is perpetuated. We see this in the conversations between Doña Josefa and her son Carlos, as well as in the comments of the overseer Don Eulogio. In the minds of these people, the black is reduced to the category of a thing, merchandise for exchange, without any sensitivity; he is merely a wild hunting dog (13, 87–88). And in fact, in Zambrada's view, slavery lowers the slave to such a state: "Slavery mutilates the soul so much that whatever virility there is in the slave's spirit is extinguished, and whatever nobility there is disappears" (19).

But the abjection of the black man touches the white man when the theme of crossbreeding and concubinage is introduced. Even Delmonte, a very secondary character in the novel but the antithesis of Carlos in his moral ideas, comes to accept this notion: "everybody," he says, "would do the same in your place, and a sin so pretty as Camila is not a great sin" (53). We are obviously faced here with an old topic of the abolitionist novel, but with a difference: here, the incestuous relationship that in many cases came about automatically is presented as possible, although it cannot be fully confirmed. The realistic author is well aware of the "anonymous paternity" that hinders absolute verification of this fact (19).

The concern to confine oneself to a real happening and to avoid the melodrama of incest points up the desire for realism that informs this story. This quality is more clearly shown when we compare Suárez's and Zambrana's novels. In the first, what was fundamentally most important was the heroic dimension of the protagonists conceived as romantic types, but in the second we find an effort to examine the characters as components of a complete picture of slavery, to determine their most salient features, and to analyze the psychological process that motivates their actions. Thus, without recourse to the scenes of bloody punishment so common in Suárez, Zambrana captures with greater objectivity and accuracy the situation of the slave and the institution that oppresses him. The relations of Camila and Francisco are developed with greater precision and detail, and even the characterization of Carlos, the young white, does not follow a simplistic conception. He is not a totally and essentially wicked person, as in Suárez y Romero: he is just a young person who has been perverted by the system and in whom we can find positive features. As such, he is able to understand his crime and join the federal forces that are fighting against those of the slave confederation (165). And finally, Camila's madness is not a phenomenon presented without forethought; it is a fact that has grown slowly in the psyche of the protagonist. As we see, the same dramatic elements that presided over the abolitionist novel are present here but in a new form: the product of a scholarly linking of causes and effects that directs the creation of the so-called realistic novel.

Zambrana has broken with romanticism stylistically also. More than anything, one notes an impassive contemplation of human beauty—white, mulatto, or black—expressed in sculptural terms. This impersonal view of beauty, with a Parnassian touch, reaches its culmination in the description of Lucy, a famous North American courtesan who is in Cuba as a lyrical actress. She is the "marble lady" (124), the "beautiful alabaster sculpture" (128), who is compared to the mulatto beauty of Camila. Elsewhere, in the physical descriptions of Camila and Francisco, we see a similar attitude. In addition, Zambrana's vocabulary and syntax reflect such an aesthetic concept. Instead of Suárez's slow and undulating prose, constructed in large paragraphs, *El negro Francisco* offers a style of unencumbered and vigorous elegance, with a preference for brief and simple sentences and very short paragraphs. Thus, the force of the prose is very different, revealing a new sensitivity.

In Zambrana's story we find some of the methods most peculiar to the *fin de siècle* art novel in Spanish America. The use of allusions and the reelaboration of literary or artistic material with scholarly cleverness are constant throughout the novel. Eve, Beatrice, Othello, Hamlet, Ophelia, Adonis, and Hercules are strung into the story, defined by a double expressive function: on the one hand, they serve as archetypes that typify the characters' physical or psychological makeup or particular state of mind; on the other hand, they serve to elevate the style of the narration and make an aesthetic impact on the reader. In addition, the clear perception of exotic interiors felt to be decadent—Carlos's Turkish-style smoking room (50), the confusion of sensory, optical, and auditory images (36), the plastic view of nature (109), and the use of sumptuous and refulgent materials (109)—gives the narrative a very turn-of-the-century tone. We are on the verge of modernism; some of its devices are discernible even in the most decidedly abolitionist moments of the story. Sugar, acquired with the blood and sweat of the slave, will be exchanged "for hides from the North, for wheat from the South, for cotton, for silk, for gold, for the lively flame of the diamond, and for the painting by Greuze or the statue by Cánova" (113). The machine house of a sugar mill is described according to a literary vision that underlies its dramatic quality: "Dante would have made of it [the machine house] a picture of his hell. The slaves, agitated, breathless, and fearful, went back and forth as if moved by strange springs, looking not like human beings but like the condemned" (147). It is beyond the scope of this study to point out to what extent Zambrana owes these elements of a new sensibility to his stay in Chile. Perhaps, like Ruben Darío some years later, the Cuban novelist was able in Santiago to put himself in touch with the European works that were to have a decisive influence on the beginnings of the Spanish-American modernist movement.

G. R. Coulthard has pointed out that the only Cuban abolitionist novel in which we find "an effort to go deep into the psychology of the Negro" and that presents black protagonists "with a well-defined racial personality" is this story by Zambrana.[7] This observation is due, in our opinion, to the two elements we have pointed out above: the author's desire for realism, on one hand, and his aestheticizing conception of beauty, on the other. The latter is very evident in the physical description of Camila:

> Someone else is there: a young mulatto woman. Her name is Camila and she is seventeen. She is strikingly beautiful. Wrapped with exquisite elegance in a long and full dressing gown, her hair covered with a little chiffon scarf, she seems to shiver in the cool morning air, and, lying rather than sitting at Doña Josefa's feet on a little bench, she has a certain nervous posture, that a painter would like to have caught, or that a cat would imitate. [12]

The author uses this attitude of sensual indolence—emphasized by tones of elegance and refinement, as well as by the catlike posture in which he visualizes the girl in her totality—to build an image of physical voluptuousness in the character, always felt in plastic terms; this image will be intensified by its assimilation to the abstract archetype of mulatto beauty, as this beauty is perceived by Zambrana: "The mulatto daughter of a white is, in physical makeup, a marvel that brings to mind the legendary sirens; the woman in which the marvel is well embodied possesses a gift superior to beauty, the gift of elegance; that is to say, she possesses that kind of spontaneous elegance that makes of cotton what can be made of velvet" (20). Notice how the mulatto woman is raised, imaginatively, to the level of a fabulous and mythical figure and how she has the faculty of changing everyday cotton into a luxurious adornment, elaborated with that style—a pleasure to the eyes because of its iridescent display of colors and to the touch because of its silky thickness—so dear to the hearts of the modernist writers. These are the qualities of Camila, who also possesses "the greatest stateliness and charm possible to the mulatto type, for, raised in luxury, she acquired without difficulty the refinement of taste and customs which are themselves beautiful and without which beauty lacks perfection" (20). This mulatto woman is a tropical "hothouse flower."

But this body, "charmingly delicate and weak," doesn't suit the young women's spirit, which is "as clear as crystal":

> There was a virgin in this siren. With such a soul she should have had a different kind of beauty. Her body seemed a charming mistake of fate. There was in her not what causes the gentle intoxication of the soul but something that kindles the frenzied drunkenness of the senses. The delicacy of her features, the feline grace of her movements, her palpitating bosom, her lips made for kisses rather than for words. . . . [47]

Camila is aware of this contradiction, and it is a severe torment to her. "She was the demon of guilty dreams, the statue of temptation, and there was such a radiance in the sweetness of her look and such luxury in her features, such sculptural vigor in her contours that instead of being a nymph, she was a bacchante" (48). Finally, the description of the girl abandoned to the erotic dreams of the siesta is more sensual, if possible:

> Camila's head was reclined on the high part of the divan and her body stretched out languidly over the seat. One foot, barely covered by a light shoe and the transparent silk she had on, showed a little under the wide skirt, because she had fallen asleep unexpectedly. Camila's right hand was resting over her heart as if defending it against impressions she feared, the other was hanging over the divan, like those wonderful hands drawn by Cellini's muse. The long velvet fringe cast a charming shadow over her face, and her slightly opened mouth appeared to offer an ideal kiss. [82]

We shall, no doubt, be pardoned for the length of the citations in view of their importance in giving evidence of Zambrana's aestheticizing tendency and of the elements of modernism that we find in his story. But this insistence on Camila's physical beauty, constant throughout the novel, also has the function of conditioning Carlos's behavior and thus the development of the plot. This powerful body "explains all the horrors of the drama" (91), because in her beauty lies the origin of her tragic destiny. In addition, this insistence, experienced gradually in many parts of the narration, exhibits Zambrana's capacity for sensing the mulatto girl's beauty and expressing her eroticism and sensuality. There has been established between the author and his character an identification that has its origin in his aesthetic enjoyment of mulatto beauty.

But Camila has more than a splendid body. We have already seen the fundamental purity and ingenuousness of her adolescent heart, which does not, I believe, assume any idealization, but we discover her psychological secret in the progressive racial consciousness the protagonist develops. Daughter of a mulatto woman slave of Doña Josefa and of a white man, possibly Doña Josefa's husband (19), Camila has been reared in the Orellana family like a señorita: "she served only her mistress, and that she did in the ways a daughter could have" (21). The girl came to forget completely that she was a slave, "and it even happened that sometimes she forgot she was a mulatto" (21) and then felt ashamed upon realizing she was one. Her first acquaintance with blackness occurs when she is struck in the midst of her inner dreams by hearing, in a conversation Doña Josefa is having with some friends, that "the difference of races is a definitive and unexceptionable obstacle in friendship and love" (27). She realizes that she must give up the "delusion of her beautiful fantasies and her chimerical dreams" (27). The memory of her mulatto mother, forgotten until now, and the presence of Francisco, the slave calash driver of the aristocratic family, begin to take on some importance to her.

Indeed, "as she became favorably disposed to the Negro race, she could not but notice the virtues of that man who was its most beautiful prototype, so strong, so heroic, so active . . . who for the love of his race had just defied a horrible and repugnant death; there at his side she would certainly be more protected than by the disdainful pity of the whites" (28). Camila therefore breaks with the false paternalism of the slave society, and her love for Francisco, which is deepening, causes her to be drawn back more and more deeply to her own other blood, the African. Through the stories the calash driver tells her about his antecedents, she identifies more deeply with "her more unlucky mother. Now she will no longer be ashamed of being a mulatto" (64).

Likewise, she will very soon come to understand the tragic fate of her mother and of the mulatto woman in general as she relives it in her own life. Carlos first offers her a shameless concubinage, and this forces her into an illicit sexual relationship. In this way, her mulatto being is illuminated for her from within as she comes to understand the background of her own birth and the fate to which she is condemned in the slave society: "Who knows whether my poor mother, whom I have sometimes blamed for what I thought was her own misconduct, who knows whether she too had to accept an imperious and omnipotent love?" (101).

On the other hand, her relationship with Francisco is the element that makes her spirit mature; but at the same time, it makes her assume her own tragic fate. Her admiration for the calash driver began as the result of his honest behavior in a little domestic incident (18) that showed her the slave's moral integrity, and the feelings he inspired in her in the dangerous moments of a trip sufficed to calm and content her (23). Thus, when she is repudiated by white society, epitomized by Doña Josefa, she inclines toward the slave, as we have seen. At first she seeks a sort of fraternal relationship, like the one she thought she had with Carlos, but when she realizes that the slave is apparently content with that kind of treatment, a special sort of melancholy begins to grow in her spirit: " 'he didn't really love me,' she says to herself, 'it's a sort of good fortune.' But this good fortune rather saddens her" (39). This small but essential psychological touch that Zambrana introduces into Camila is the first amorous impulse shown in the beautiful mulatto. The love process has begun in her.

This passion begins to take on form and intensity in the young woman. She cannot bear the calash driver's well-feigned indifference; "she would have preferred frank hatred to the indifference he showed toward her" (40). So the naive Camila feels wounded in the depths of her pride, which pushes her to play the game and fight the battle of the sexes in the love relationship. She employs the weapons of the most refined coquetry: her voice, when she speaks to Francisco, becomes a "melancholy cooing"; her glance is fixed on him "sweetly and caressingly"; she surrounds him with "enchantments," producing in him "the fever of passion, the wreck of all his strong resolutions on the wave of fire that enveloped his thoughts and his feelings" (40). We are witnessing a detailed psychological analysis of the initial phase in the love relationship between a man and a woman. This battle of the sexes will be maintained until the relationship reaches its climax; the beautiful mulatto wants, in her very feminine way, to prolong "the period of her dominion, her fleeting reign, her right of conquest" (59), before pronouncing "the 'I love you' that was hovering around her lips" (59). But once these words have been proffered, coquetry gives way to "a very lively emotion, as she gave herself over unreservedly to the feeling Francisco's passion had caused to germinate in her soul" (62). This novice's love, like a vertigo at first, will gradually evolve into a confidence in the future whose fulcrum is the beloved's being. Camila has found her man and has satisfied her womanly instinct (62).

Camila's realization of her feminine and ethnic potential is the result, therefore, of the love relationship she begins with Francisco. The calash driver, "that strange creature from the jungle" (22), had been sold as a slave when he was twelve years old. His compatriots, understanding his origins, respected his ancestral line, but for the white novelist this ancestry is really a mystery, since "A negro slave rarely speaks in the white's presence of his homeland, or of what has happened there, first because he does not consider it prudent and then because he judges it to be a kind of profanation" (21). Thus, Zambrana is very consicous of the difficulty encountered in creating a character of this type. The "tribal" black raises a barrier to white penetration; his hidden being is a jealously guarded mystery. The novelist, then, has to create a psychology that is more a result of the author's own intuition and cautious observation than a product of an unattainable knowledge of the ultimate being of these men. But this acknowledgment and honest posing of the problem are the first steps in its solution. Suárez y Romero had handled it by making his Francisco an absolutely unique being; Zambrana will try to give his character two dimensions—that of his own individuality, like any human being, and that of the culture in which he has his roots.

The point of departure is the differentiation, physical and psychological, that the novelist establishes between the blacks born on the island and the African; Francisco, although he has a good face, "is not effeminate like the colonial Negroes from Havana" (16). From the beginning, Zambrana underlines a virility that slavery has not been able to strike out of this character, a virility—not machismo—expressed by his serene courage in the face of danger, which seems to come to him from his ancestry of primitive men faced with the constant dangers of "jungle" life. Handsome, "somewhat rustic," he seemed "a prisoner of civilization":

Francisco was a strong man. He had the vigor that is bodily strength and the pride that is strength of the soul. Looking at him, one understood that he was incapable of vacillation in the presence of an obstacle, and that probably he had never felt the ice of fear in his nerves, in the face of any kind of danger. He was an Apollo of ebony; his head was proudly set, he had broad shoulders, a powerful chest, he stood on the ground as if on a pedestal, and one could see in his eyes that he was no less robust inside than outwardly. He had muscles of steel and a heart of granite. [23]

As we can clearly see, Zambrana could appreciate black beauty.

The first hint we get of Francisco's character and behavior is the moral integrity he shows when he is accused obliquely of having stolen the gold place setting and the money bag (15). This action gives the author a basis for introducing the opposing opinions of the slave held by Doña Josefa and Carlos. For her, the calash driver is an insolent savage, simply because he was not born in Cuba (15–16). Her son thinks, on the contrary, that Francisco is rather intelligent and basically very humble (16). But this humility is relative: in reality, Francisco accepts slavery as a "perquisite" of the war between enemy tribes, bearing it like a "stoic warrior": "He accepted the respect of his compatriots as a just homage, and offered the whites the forms of his respect, which they had bought in a trade not entirely illicit in the eyes of him who had been its victim" (22). Francisco has a primitive and elemental view of slavery: he suffers under it, he is aware of it and conscious of the limits it imposes on his existence, and yet he sees a certain logic in it. He regards slavery, not as an institution viewed in the abstract, but as a perquisite derived from the law of the jungle. And he nevertheless feels a nostalgia for that life, "a bitter patriotism" that consists in loving "barbarism, the dark, and the unfortunate" (22).

The racial consciousness of this character is based on an irrational pride in his blood and on an identification with the magicomystical world of African tribalism. The first of these characteristics can be seen in his relationship with Camila. Francisco feels that what the young woman is doing—proposing to quit her race—is an "unpardonable crime" (22), because he considers himself "the representative, proud, intransigent, savage, of the Negro race" (23). The second

characteristic is evident in his indelible memory of the life he had
led in his country and in the ritual celebrations in which he partici-
pates and with which he feels himself fully identified:

> he and his companions used to assemble periodically to cele-
> brate the strange and fantastic rites prescribed by the religion
> of their forefathers, and then one of the Negro elders would
> tell a story of the fatherland in a song he had composed. A
> melancholy refrain, intoned by everyone at the end of each
> verse the old cantor psalmodized, invariably contained the
> theme of the narration in one vigorous phrase. [63]

Besides remaining within the limits of its African ambit, the characterization of Francisco has very specific elements of primitivism.
We have pointed out Zambrana's comprehension of slavery, but we
may also notice the emphasis he puts into contrasting the "refined
orderliness of Camila" with "that rough nature rebellious against
culture" that characterizes the black calash driver. In Francisco, we
also see the confusion between civilization and barbarism, shown
in the primitive form of his love for the mulatto woman. When he
experiences wild jealousy, he is the victim of a frightening vision:
"he could imagine himself just as well behind a tree as behind a
wall" lying in ambush with a dagger in his hand that, pushed by
some strange force, was being sunk into the chest of a man whose
blood pouring out "awoke in him the most delicious impression he
had experienced in his life" (72). And the fact is that, in Francisco's
"harsh nature, which has not been modified by good rearing, there
is a vehemence which makes of love, jealousy, revenge, and remorse
veritable hurricanes of the soul" (34).

These are the elements that govern his relationship with Camila.
The first feeling he had had toward her was apparently one of deep
repugnance—"that mulatto woman, mixed up with the whites, inspired a profound aversion in him" (23)—but in his way, he had
loved her for a long time. "She inspired almost hate in him, but
there are hatreds which require nothing more than to become an
unbridled passion" (36). Therefore, when the brown girl turns toward
the black world, at the same time revealing the tenderness she feels
toward him, love blooms intensely in the slave, as does its correlate,
jealousy (71). The depiction of this love gives us a better understand-

ing of the psychology of the hero, because Francisco sees Camila from the point of view of a black. For the slave, the mulatto woman is not just the image of sensuality and voluptuousness incarnated in a magnificent body, as she is for Carlos; although he is very sensitive to the "influence of her prodigious physical charm, which makes him suffer without understanding it at all" (56), Francisco senses "the delight of looking into Camila's eyes" (56) and being enamored of her nature. And this is what conquers the girl, definitively. The calash driver is the first man to have sensed in her something more than an instrument of his pleasure. The mulatto girl has encountered a human response, even though it be in a "Negro, in a savage, in a slave" (56).

As in Suárez y Romero, the protagonists will fulfill their tragic destiny through this love that unites them. On the one hand, Doña Josefa prohibits Camila from marrying the black man (66); on the other hand, Camila faces the eroticism of Carlos (69). The mulatto will give herself to Carlos to save the slave; Francisco, seeing that his love "no longer can be," commits suicide (162); Camila dies insane (163). But suicide and insanity are sensed and treated very differently here than in Suárez y Romero. Here there is no romantic desperation; Francisco simply hangs himself. The author believes he has shown the process and depth of Francisco's love with sufficient clarity and detail that its frustration will very naturally lead to death. Having done this, he feels that no embellishment is necessary. As for Camila, this is not "a death from sadness," as in Dorotea; it is a madness that has gestated gradually and that at this point does not seem improbable or melodramatic. Camila's ideas have become "confused" ever since she has had to face Carlos (142); later, the physical punishment inflicted on Francisco leaves her "unaware, cold, almost senseless" (146); then she suffers convulsions and her ideas no longer "will be linked together in a perfect chain" (147); and, at last, when she realizes that defeat is inevitable, "the smile of the insane Ophelia began to play over her lips" (150). And so we come back to where we began our analysis. The greater effort toward realism and the new sensibility apparent in Zambrana's style and literary aesthetic permitted him to create two beings that go beyond classification as means to an end or type. With Francisco and Camila, the cycle of abolitionist novels comes to a close, but if the slave as a character in the contemporary narrative disappears with them, some of the psychological elements derived from this endeavor to penetrate the black soul will reappear in later black or mulatto protagonists.

II   Ramón Meza: *Carmela*

Just as *El negro Francisco* by Antonio Zambrana finds its point of departure in the earlier novel by Anselmo Suárez y Romero, it has been said more than once that *Carmela* (1886) by Ramón Meza y Suárez Inclán (1861–1911) is "a younger sister of *Cecilia Valdés*." [8] This judgment may have a semblance of truth only if we limit ourselves to a mechanical comparison of the basic plots of the two novels. In fact, Meza's novel, like Villaverde's, has as its feminine protagonist an almost white mulatto girl involved in a love relationship with a young man from the economic aristocracy; in both novels, the relationship leads to a catastrophic denouement; and finally, one can see a certain similarity in the parallel arrangement of the social levels on which the action is developed in both novels. But a deeper analysis of the texts reveals radical differences. Villaverde's basic intention was to point up the corruption in the slave society; thus, the concubinage of Cecilia was the product of an elemental passion that found its course and was carried out due to the inferior position of the mulatto girl. Carmela and Joaquín, on the contrary, love each other sincerely, and they have recourse to the illicit sexual relationship as a means of achieving marriage. The young white does not deceive the mulatto girl; his wish is to marry her, a wish that is gradually destroyed by the racial prejudices of his family.

In addition, Cecilia is without caste in a society made up of rich colonial *hacendados,* colonial chamberlains and administrators, and a huge mass of blacks and slaves. Carmela, on the contrary, belongs to the bourgeoisie, is accepted by them, and could have married a man of the same social level as she. The fiestas given for her by Doña Justa, her feigned godmother, and the sympathy with which the young woman is received are proof of this fact. Meza's intent is very different from Villaverde's: his concern centers in ethnic prejudice, more and more acute as one advances in social levels. Whites and blacks mix in the lower classes, mulattoes are accepted by the bourgeoisie, and they find themselves discriminated against by the aristocracy of money or of family.

In addition to these thematic differences, the style and narrative technique of the two writers are very different. Villaverde is, as we have noted, a *costumbrista* concerned with local color and with "types" and social mores, as evidenced in the inventorylike ennumeration that pervades *Cecilia Valdés*. His novel is a juxtaposition of pictures, some of them unnecessary and annoying. The structure of *Cecilia Valdés* is zigzag, repetitive, and often incoherent. In *Carmela* we have a much less ambitious novel but a more successful and harmonious one. Villaverde's influence might have been thematic, although his subject matter was a commonplace in Cuban society. Meza's technique, on the other hand, approaches Don Benito Pérez Galdós, and in some descriptive methods he is close to Emile Zola.[9] Villaverde's style is deliberately archaic in its vocabulary, with a very complicated syntax and an abundance of grammatical errors, whereas Meza's style is abbreviated, direct, and simple and shows some of the techniques of modernist prose, especially in the use of elements of plastic beauty and brilliance, although to a lesser degree than in Zambrana. In Meza's novel, we find such expressions as "phosphorescent lights," "opal vapours," "the moon silvered the water like a dazzling and restless silver mesh," or "the red damask curtain with golden galloons, which the light of the restless candles seem to set on fire." The figure of the Asiatic character, Assam, allows Meza to bring in the world of Chinese trinkets and the various Japanese things so much enjoyed by the modernist movement, and in general there is fine perception of enclosed, refined, and elegant interiors.

We have intentionally made this parallel between Villaverde and Meza extensive so as to point up the value of the aesthetics that enliven Meza's novel. *Carmela* and his better known story, *Mi tío el empleado* (1887), a satirical and caricatural view of Cuban society in the period of liquidation of the colonial administration, are excellent examples of the realistic novel in Spanish America that we should rescue from the relative oblivion in which they are buried.

Another notable difference between these novels lies in the characterization of the feminine protagonist. Cecilia is a character with a static psychology, and her behavior is unchanging throughout the story. But in Carmela, we sense growth, development of temperament, and a consequent evolution in motivation and behavior. We witness a process of maturing, human and feminine, dominated by the character's ever sharper and clearer sense of ethnic awareness. As she awakens to this consciousness and realizes the social implications it carries with it, Carmela achieves her ultimate identity, at the same time relating herself to her authentic origin. In this sense, she will follow a course similar to that of Camila, although the force that motivates her is different.

Carmela is very light-skinned, the daughter of a quadroon, Doña Justa, and a Spanish merchant whose name the mother never cared to remember. At birth, Carmela "was a beautiful little girl, almost pure blooded, a perfect delight" for both parents,[10] but after three years of happy concubinage, the Spaniard abandons his temporary and improvised family, having left them sufficient fortune to maintain a decent and comfortable standard of living. At the beginning of the story, Doña Justa, Carmela, and a black servant they called Tocineta ("Fatty") because of his obesity live in a comfortable house on San Lazaro Avenue. The episode with the Spaniard having been forgotten, Doña Justa presents her daughter as her godchild.

Everyone accepts the young woman as a white, at least officially, although there is some surreptitious comment about her mixed blood, especially among the servants in the neighborhood. Our protagonist has never heard this, because all her friends accept her as an equal. Carmela, although she did not possess "the classical contours of the Greek Venus, was a model of plastic beauty" (5):

> Her hair, black and shiny as ebony, if a little crisp and short, fell in thick tresses onto her shoulders. Her arched eyebrows and long, curled lashes lightly shaded her brilliant black eyes. . . . she was of medium height: slightly broad shoulders, slightly fleshy arms, a narrow waist, but the lines of her robust and agile body were well proportioned, making such a pleasant figure. [4–5]

In this physical description of the character, there is only one doubtful feature that might point to the presence of African blood in her veins: the slightly "crisp" hair. Hence, Carmela considers herself a white and, in the social circle in which she is growing up, she feels secure and admired for her beauty. She fears nothing, nor has she any reason to feel uneasy. Her "little mother" is a magnificent protectress, her seaside house a delight of order and comfort, and it is only occasionally that she feels too strongly the monotony of her existence. Her accidental acquaintance with Joaquín crowns her joy.

The love relationship between these two begins in all the naiveté of adolescence. Carmela blushes constantly and feels an almost childish joy when she sees Joaquín, who comes courting her every day. At the fiesta where he will be presented to Doña Justa and where the couple will be together for the first time, Carmela's face is "a little rosier than usual; in the agitation of her bosom and her uneasy look, one could see that she was full of the impatience of a person who is waiting anxiously" (21). Here we have the image of a timid young woman in love, who is being initiated in the game of the sexes. There is nothing resembling the jealousy and unbridled passion traditionally attributed to the mulatto woman. At the party, Carmela behaves like a white, middle-class señorita: "she had on a white percale dress with pink lace decorations, the pleats and tucks of which emphasized very artfully her tall and elegant stature, while she walked proud and content in front of a mirror in the living room, with a certain jaunty and provocative gait" (21). But it is precisely at that party that the dramatic element of the narrative is introduced: the servants who have accompanied their masters there mention Carmela's "mulattoness" when they see how well she follows the rhythm of the colonial dance. "That girl, they said from behind Tocineta, you can really tell that girl has the blood of a . . ." (34).

Moreover, as a result of this same party, of which she has been the undisputed queen, Carmela will fall into a sea of caviling and questioning. She begins now to notice the difference in her social class with respect to Joaquín's. "What worried her most was the idea of asking Joaquín how he had liked the party. She felt certain scruples on account of the inferiority of the social sphere in which she and her *mamita* lived, as compared with the level of the young man and his family" (68). And when this love comes upon her, she wonders for the first time who she is: "Her godmother, *mamita*, served her as both mother and father, but this, although it was sufficient for her, was not enough to define the place she should take in society" (68).

As we see, the idea of the racial problem has not yet occurred to the protagonist, but she is beginning to sense that her situation is a bit irregular. It is her sentimental relationship with Joaquín that makes her leave, if only psychologically at first, the artificial protection under which she has lived thus far. The love affair therefore has a social consequence, and she "who seemed like a white young lady" (69) will begin to have full awareness of the differences, including the ethnic ones, that limit her and define her as a person.

As she begins to be aware of these social differences, however, she initiates the process of maturing as a woman. Carmela is able to live in her dream world until one morning when Doña Justa has a luncheon for Joaquín. At the table, Joaquín does not know what to do. He feels very uneasy about the free and easy manners of the "godmother" and the "godchild" and even about the menu, a typical middle-class meal, and he never can understand the kind of ingenuousness and familiarity that allows Carmela to "violate the table manners," that is, to use her hands to eat the delicious shellfish and corn mush. All this makes a striking contrast with the stiff, courtly manners of his own home, it all seems strange to him and, to a certain degree, repugnant. Therefore, when his father, Don Julián, invades the San Làzaro house, the boy does not know how to behave. He becomes a silent statue (112), an automaton (118), and he thinks only of his humiliation. Because of this humiliation, he resolves to flee with Carmela in order later to be obliged to marry her.

But Carmela has understood very well from the heated conversation between Doña Justa and Don Julián that she is not equal to Joaquín, that he could not present her to society (114–16), and that she is really Doña Justa's daughter (117). She has also realized who Joaquín is, "understanding how little she could pin her hopes any longer on his resolutions" (127). But her childhood and adolescent world has fallen to the ground so rapidly that she is not yet able to replace it with an adult view of life. Carmela "didn't realize exactly what had happened, even though she had seen and heard it all, and what she had not seen and heard, she had perhaps guessed" (126).

Therefore, when Joaquín proposes an elopement to Marianao, she accepts because she is still naive enough to believe in a marriage that is impossible from any point of view, ethnically or socially. Up to this time, their relationship has been idyllic, as we could see from their attitudes before the tragic luncheon that changed the course of their lives (103–5), but once their love is consummated in the sexual act, what might have been an idyll becomes a tragedy. This tragedy has its source not only in social circumstances but also in the very nature and circumstances of their love. Although they are sincere and apparently in love with one another, "they had not found that limitless joy, that ineffable pleasures they had dreamed of" (143). As we see, sex defrauds them.

This becomes evident in Carmela, who wants "to go back home to her *mamita*" (144), and when she returns to Doña Justa's side, the second cycle of crossbreeding and abandonment begins. The god-mother cannot keep up her own deceit; an acute awareness of the identification of her fate with that of her daughter prevents it. Thus, in Carmela we see fulfilled once again the topical fate of the mulatto woman—abandoned by her father and her lover and prevented from achieving a high position in established society. Through the words of Doña Justa, this idea is emphasized: "Yes, you are my daughter! I was seduced like you, my daughter, and you have not seen your father at your side" (147).

The definitive oblivion to which Joaquín condemns her when he is sent to the United States by his father, and the son born as a result of the relationship, cause Carmela to mature both physically and psychologically. After a two-year stay in a town near Havana where she has gone to conceal her pregnancy, "she returned radiantly beautiful; she was at the height of her beauty" (165). From this time on, there is a radical change in her behavior. She overcomes the scruples she has had against becoming betrothed to the rich Chinese merchant, Juan Cipriano Assam, because of the satisfaction she has in dominating the Asian and because of the economic and social significance of the marriage. Now we are coming close to the traditional image of the mulatto woman: calculating, sensual, and vengeful. Her delights grow daily, "and they were heightened by the magnificient gowns, finery, and jewelry that the prodigal hand of the liberal Asian provided for her" (186).

Carmela, with Doña Justa's help, has succeeded in "arranging everything": the baby passes for her nephew, the splendor of days past has returned to the house on San Lázaro, and the girl is on the verge of obtaining a solid and definitive position in the petit-bourgeois society in which she is flourishing (188). But Joaquín's return to Havana to get married gradually knocks down this structure of apparent tranquillity, so laboriously built. Carmela has continued to love him secretly, "she had not forgotten him, she could never forget him" (188); but what activates the mechanism of jealousy and revenge in the mulatto woman is not only her love but also her ethnic and social resentment: "The most rabid jealousy awoke suddenly in Carmela. . . . Joaquín disdained her for one reason, for just one reason, . . . because he considered her racially inferior" (191).

As we see, the erotic relationship, when its process is complete, causes the character to assume her racial status, and this essentially mulatto behavior of the protagonist forms the climax of the novel. It is in this feature that the stories by Villaverde and Meza have the greatest similarity, but it is here also that we note more clearly the differences between the two novelists. As with Cecilia Valdés, Carmela's revenge takes place at the time of the marriage, specifically in the church; but unlike the first novel, this time there is no recourse to violence. There are no daggers, no blood; what the young mulatto girl plans is a social scandal with which she intends to destroy the reputation of her lover's family. At this moment, the girl's tragic destiny is transformed, as it hurries to its final consequences: "The young girl felt faint; she had not the courage to do what she had intended to do; she had lost her wits; dark circles appeared around her eyes; her body shook and shook; over her forehead as cold as marble ran a cool, fine sweat; her hands trembled, and her black, crisp, uncombed hair had fallen into uneven locks" (197).

In the "physiological" description of the heroine's physical and emotional state—in which Carmela's one differentiating ethnic feature appears for the second and last time—we can see that in both appearance and behavior she assumes the image of the mulatto. But this image is psychological and behavioral rather than a reflection of external racial appearance. Carmela, according to her own graphic expression, has "violated table manners"—that is, she has broken with the social customs, lowering herself in the scale of Cuban social classes. She has therefore become a member of Doña Justa's class. When the priest asks about impediments to the marriage of Joaquín and Luisa and Carmela breaks forth in "a sharp cry, in a roar like a wounded lioness" (197), those present at the elegant ceremony pretend to take her for what she seems to be, a madwoman or a drunk (198). Abandoned by Assam and destroyed both psychologically and socially, she has no other recourse after Doña Justa's death than to unite with the black Tocineta (205).

It is evident that in Carmela we have had to utilize the organization of the plot to characterize the black protagonist. This is due to the fact that in this narrative the protagonist is seen from the outside, behaving basically as a reflection of a definite social situation that almost always forms a framework. The mulatto's behavior is a chain reaction to an environment; before the prejudices of the moneyed aristocracy have acted upon her, she is a young white girl belonging to the petit bourgeoisie. What has changed is the way this society functions, and with it the character's social reaction; the psychology, in its general lines, remains the same. Meza's merit lies in indicating the mental process that culminates in this last state, although its understanding by the novelist continues to be in large measure topical. If the characterization of the mulatto girl in *Cecilia Valdés* is an unalterable figure with rigid lines, in *Carmela* it is an embryo that has not completed its development. Nevertheless, it demonstrates a deepening in the concept of the mulatto woman.

This advance in the concept of the black character is most obvious in the secondary characters of the novel, Doña Justa and Tocineta. Manuel de la Cruz has observed that Meza develops this kind of figure "with the hand of a master," [11] and Carmela's feigned godmother is an excellent corroboration of this assertion. When the story begins, Doña Justa is about fifty years old, and "certain lines on her forehead, a languidness in her look, and more than anything, a laxness in her movements and the stifled sighs she kept emitting, gave evidence that she carried some hidden anxiety in her heart" (10–11). This secret anxiety is her abandonment by the Spaniard to whom she had entrusted the hopes of her youth. To overcome her feeling of personal frustration, the mulatto woman dedicates herself to religious practices and to the education of the "godchild," Carmela. At her first appearance, we see her saying the rosary: "The robust silhouette of Doña Justa was seen kneeling with religious unction before the Bronze Virgin of Charity. . . . She was both her most indefatigable priestess and her most constant devotee" (9).

But we would deceive ourselves if we placed this interesting character in the same category as Chepilla, the grandmother of Cecilia Valdés. The only point of contact between the two women is this mystical propensity, a means of escape for a personality traumatized by deceit and oblivion. But for Seña Josefa this is the only possibility of overcoming an adverse and immediate reality whereas, Doña Justa, who develops in a more favorable environment, will on the contrary, try to transform it and adapt it to her own existence.

In fact, before being seduced, Doña Justa had belonged in a special way to the high society of Havana. "Taken in" by a family of the

Cuban aristocracy, she has acquired the manners and customs of high society, which she tries to reproduce in her circle on San Lázaro Avenue. In order to achieve this objective, she has to construct a fantasy that will become her own reality. So, well acquainted with ethnic prejudice and racial discrimination, more and more acute as one advances socially, Doña Justa will not accept the idea that she is a mulatto. She considers herself a white woman. The pretentious parties she gives have a double function: to find a match for Carmela on a higher social level and to obtain the social prestige she so desires: "Other more cruel and irresponsible gossips said that Doña Justa gave the parties in order to rub elbows with people of a higher class than she, because for some distance around, it was known that she wanted to pass for a white without being one" (20).

When Joaquín is presented to her at one of these parties, Doña Justa, who in her imagination lives in the high society to which this wealthy heir's family belongs (bear in mind that she makes a pretense of knowing all about the marriages and relations of the most important Havana families), "came to imagine, and finally to convince herself that she knew the young man's parents and grandparents very well, which filled Carmela with delight" (24). And just as the girl has firmly believed the foregoing, because of the aplomb and the firmness with which her "mamita" has directed the conversation, she also accepts her status as godchild, as does everyone else. Doña Justa has created a new reality out of her imagination with which she hopes to avoid having Carmela "pay for the only mistake of her life, committed under the influence of a single ardent and sincere passion" (41). The character thus shows herself to be a master in the art of manipulating social conventions and arranging them to her own advantage.

Here we are obviously seeing another dimension of the mulatto nature. Up to this point, the mulatto character, particularly the woman, has yielded to a set of generally elementary and primitive passions, which guide her blindly toward a catastrophic end. Like Zambrana's Camila, Meza's Doña Justa surpasses the common "bronze Venus" concept and gives us a view of the mulatto woman who functions not only by means of coarse calculation or indecent sex but with the idea of survival in a society pervaded by ethnic prejudice. And what concerns us is the novelist's success in having endowed Doña Justa with a defense mechanism, which is, precisely, her own fantasy and imagination. This makes for greater coherence in the characterization, because the mulatto girl is not concerned, like an arriviste, in ascending the social ladder; for her this movement is almost instinctive, a natural impulse that springs from her deepest dreams. There is no calculation; what shows in the mamita is a clear sense of mimicry. Out of habit, she knows the mulatto must be integrated to the white if she wants to survive. And Doña Justa's art is in this capacity to appear white without being authentically white.

It is because of this that she accepts as natural the incipient love relationship between Carmela and Joaquín, for their marriage would be the logical end of this world of dreams. Even when Don Julián appears in her house with the object of provoking a crisis, she does not feel the slightest change; "she had become so accustomed to maintaining the illusion of her self-deceit that she thought everyone else was deceived" (116). But the reality she has tried so hard to push aside ends by striking her hard in the face. First, Carmela's dishonor brings forth the natural confession from her motherly heart (146); then Assam's abandonment of her daughter and the collapse of all her fantasies bring her to her death (201). But out of these conflicts, the character still puts together the broken pieces of her dreams; the baby will become the nephew of the godchild, the fiestas will return, things will be "fixed up again," and in the house on San Lázaro Avenue it is as if nothing had happened. Once she finds out that everyone knows what has happened, she will cease to exist (201).

This constant interplay of dreams, fantasy, and reality in the mind of Doña Justa is what imparts the greatest interest to the characterization. It is the product of what might be called a mulatto psychology conditioned by the social environment and the pretense it requires. The transformation that reality undergoes in the mulatto woman's psyche is based on an inner desire to create a new reality in which ethnic and social differences have disappeared for her and for her godchild, although they are maintained with respect to certain other individuals, such as Tocineta. Thus, there is a desire to erase all class consciousness in herself, an obsession with appearing "pure-blooded," and hence the disdain with which she treats the black servant. But at the same time she feels an inner uneasiness, for she realizes she does not in fact belong to the privileged class. Here we have an intensification of the inner conflict we found in Villaverde's characterization. Cecilia Valdés disdained the black man because she wanted to have white children; Doña Justa looks down on him in order to feel white and "superior"; for Carmela who thinks she is "pure," Tocineta is simply a black man. The tragedy of Doña Justa is in acting out her racial "purity," a tragedy that Carmela has unwittingly inherited.

Contrasted with these pretentious characters, the figure of Tocineta, the servant, shows a simple and elementary sense of existence. In the presence of others, he behaves as if in terror, his personality taking on the features of a still, carnival figure. His real figure contributes to the image, "a young and very fat Negro, his fatness the reason for the nickname that completely replaced his real one" (10). When his mistress exhibits him to her friends, the poor, dark fellow feels so panicky that his features, paralyzed with terror, make him look almost like an imbecile "without any facial expression showing wits, subtlety, or even the mischievousness usually found in Negroes his age" (35).

The character's social behavior reflects an elementary psychology that is revealed in his private existence, either by means of little details—feeding the rabbits, mounting a horse in a stupid way—or in the secret passion he feels for Carmela, which shapes his life. The black man's silent love for the mulatto girl can be noted from the beginning of the narrative. For example, when he sees the two lovers, Carmela and Joaquín, dancing, "He watched avidly the motions and turns Carmela made in the dance. At times his hands became stiff and pressed hard on back of the chair he was leaning against" (35). The frustration he feels changes to violent, formless jealousy when he relives the scene he has just beheld in the privacy of his own room: "perhaps painful thoughts or sinister ideas tormented the unhappy African, for he ground his teeth, he struck the window-casing with his fists, and his eyes shone with flashes of anger" (42). But this elemental explosion of the darkest forces of his being finds a palliative and a direction when he gives himself over to the playing of a primitive African instrument, a marímbula he has made himself. "Then he seemed more tranquil. . . . Afterward, he tied a madras kerchief onto his head, sat down on the window sill with his legs hanging out, and began to extract from his rough instrument strange combinations of notes, savage rhythms that sounded melancholy, sad, lugubrious, mournful in the silence of the night" (42). We can see how his own wounded sensibilities are soothed by the catharsis of playing African rhythms; but we also see how in the act of putting on the madras kerchief, typical mark of the "tribal" blacks, he shows a desire to remain firmly attached to his tribal roots. It is an act of racial pride, or at least Tocineta seems to perceive it as one in his primitive psychology, as against the contrary attitude of Doña Justa and Carmela. We find repeated in the servant a feature we have already observed in Zambrana's Francisco.

Nevertheless, Tocineta himself realizes that just because he is black he cannot aspire to the girl's love. When he watched her playing the piano, "he suffered horribly . . . with the admiration a fanatic has for his idol, without daring to show it, as if the black color of his skin took away his ability to think and love freely" (69). And, again, he rebels inwardly as he looks at himself in a mirror: "Why did he have to be a Negro? Yes, sir, why? And even if this was so, were not all men the children of God? Why couldn't she love him, who could dive from the terrace onto the seashore reefs in exchange for a kiss?" (61). This is a very elementary way of posing the problem, and on the other hand, it is revealing of the very simple psychology of this black man.

Tocineta's aversion and jealousy toward Joaquín will be duplicated in his feelings toward Assam, considering that the black man senses that there is a real possibility of marriage between Carmela and the wealthy Assam. Moreover, curiously, Tocineta manifests a racist attitude toward the Chinese, and this unlocks the mechanism that brings on the final tragedy. By informing Carmela that Joaquín has come back and is going to marry Luisa, Tocineta provokes Carmela's jealousy, Assam's suicide, and Doña Justa's death (187–89). The beautiful mulatto woman now has no other recourse; she will marry the black man, who offers her protection. It is at this moment that the full store of tenderness and kindness in the servant is revealed: "Carmela looked at him, and her look, grown wiser because of her experience, made her recognize the great sincerity of the poor, despised Tocineta . . . she approached the Negro, who opened his arms, pressed her against his chest, and planted on her smooth forehead a fervent kiss" (204).

It is symbolic that Carmela, forgotten by a white and despised by an Asian, finds refuge in this black man. He loves, perhaps in an elemental way, but in a way we could term realistic. Unlike Joaquín, who would be ashamed socially of Carmela, or Assam, who could not admit the least infidelity, Tocineta's love is essential and deep, because he accepts the girl as she is. He can wait, loving objectively and without social considerations of any kind. The merit in Meza's characterization of this black man lies in having made him inwardly pleasing while succeeding in making the reader accept very alien moral values.

III   Martín Morúa Delgado: *Sofía*

With *Sofía* (1891) by Martín Morúa Delgado (1857–1910), the first novel in which slavery is a historical phenomenon, "naturalism is introduced into Cuban literature." [12] This fact will influence decisively the organization of the principal character and the construction of the plot. In this first part of a series intended to be the story of a Cuban family,[13] it is evident that the author follows closely the plan and technique employed by Emile Zola (1840–1903) in *Les Rougon-Macquart* (1871). On the other hand, Morúa was the son of slaves, although he was born free because his parents had bought their freedom "before he came into the world," [14] and he had direct knowledge of the slave system.

Trained in naturalism, Morúa Delgado reduced the imaginative element to a minimum, giving great importance to observation. Thus, the novel takes place in the writer's native city, where his political activity gave him an intimate knowledge of the social classes. Moreover, his observation is applied above all to the psychic reality of the characters, some of whom—Magdalena Unzúazo, for example—are models of penetration. In *Sofía*, reality is described in all its minute details, with insistence on its most disagreeable aspects, among these, of course, prostitution, as it appears in Manuela Corrales, mother of the protagonist.[15] The scientistic writing of the naturalist novelists is also evident here in the detailed descriptions of sicknesses and in the relish with which Morúa creates types from the realm of the psychopathological, such as Fico Unzúazo and Rafael Arteaga. Finally, the determinism characteristic of the French naturalists shows itself in the principal character, Sofía who, although biologically a white, behaves and reacts like a mulatto slave, for that is the social status in which she lives and by which she is conditioned. The author is experimenting with two ideas: first, that society and heredity—ethnic heredity is not implied here—condition the individual, and second, that racial differences do not exist, because a white placed in the same circumstances as a black and subject to the same influences and stimuli reacts in the same way as the black.

The action of the novel takes place in Matanzas, almost immediately after the war between Cuba and Spain (1878). It was a time of hope and uncertainty, and the narrative reflects the principal problems faced by the Cuban society of the period, especially the abolition of the slave system and the incorporation of the black masses into national life. The intent of the story is to show the conversion of the plantation colony into a democratic state, in which the former slaves a d their descendants will play an important part. It follows that Moria Delgado's ultimate purpose is to emphasize the capacity of the blacks for their new function as citizens. That is what the author has in mind when, through his character Eladisloa Gonzaga, he assails the racial prejudice created by slavery and the pseudoscience that attempted to justify it:

> This argument that pseudoscience hands out to the multitudes who neither study nor read anything must have brought many pesos to the coffers of those who had an interest in the trade in human beings. Do you believe that while preaching the equality of intellectual development among blacks and whites in similar circumstances it would have been possible to propagate premeditated social inequality in such a way as later to set up the status of slave for some and master for others? [122]

The above is a summary of Morúa Delgado's thought, and that is what he wanted to experiment with in the novel. Although she is of white blood, Sofía's psychology and destiny do not differ from that of other slaves placed in the same environment, because it is the slave system, not the ethnic condition of the blacks, that keeps them in a state of abjection and ignorance, subject to the whim of masters who are themselves contaminated by the immorality of the system. In the final analysis, then, this novel is directed toward combating ethnic prejudices based on race or class superiority.

The protagonist, whom everyone takes for a mulatto woman, is a symbolic victim of the sad state of affairs created by slavery. This function is clearly evident when her life ends: "Innocence was paying its tribute to evil. Vice and depravity engendered by an infernal system, were adding another victim to the immense catalog of their degrading lapses. Sofía had ceased to be" (244). The creation of this character is determined by an extraliterary factor: the illustration of a message that is the theme of the story. The falseness of this character results not from the apparent unlikeliness of her situation[16] but from the function given her that conditions her a priori in the author's mind, obliging her to move about in the text like a sort of automaton, used as a mechanism for verifying an ideology. Morúa has based the creation of his protagonist on an idea. The weakness this brings about in Sofía is deplorably more noticeable if we compare the young slave girl with other types, so successfully depicted by this author. In contrast to the psychological study made of Magdalena or Ana María, the inner characterization of the principal character seems puerile, incomplete, and superficial. Sofía's authentic outlines are never quite perceived by the reader.

The character shows the author's disposition to idealize, from the first physical description he makes of her. "There was one swarthy brunette who stood out on account of the peaceful disposition and gentle manners that heightened her natural beauty; for Sofía was a very attractive girl. Her slightly more than medium height, one of those eternally youthful statues, accentuated a long, well-formed waist, and shoulders set so gracefully that they formed a perfect torso" (12). And the author goes on in this way, taking delight in all the remaining components of the girl's anatomy, among which stand out the "fine features" of her face and the two eyes with black pupils that "poured out torrents of tenderness." Finally, her "habitual sadness" added charm to her total appearance. We find no noticeable negroid features in her; only her swarthiness suggests the "inferior" race. And yet she is believed to belong to it; everyone looks upon her as a mulatto. The author is telling us that assigning a person to a certain race depends more on his social level than on his ethnic features. He is pointing out the existence of a doubtful "gray" segment of the population, whose individual members can be taken for whites or blacks, each according to his economic and social situation. In this case, Sofía is a mulatto because of her status as a slave. Nevertheless, the author must be faithful to a narrative technique based on "observation of nature," and so he must start at the beginning of the novel to prepare the reader for the denouement—the fact that Sofía is biologically a white. Indeed, "the little Negro girls and mulattoes who were of a deeper color took her for a white" (12–13); in the provincial town everyone agrees that Magdalena and Sofía "seemed more like sisters than like mistress and slave" (53); and Señor Nudoso del Tronco thinks "that the girl looked too much like his three children" (78).

Sofía's physical beauty and the instruction she has received from her mistress, Magdalena, give her the appearance of "a young woman of humble family, raised 'in the Holy fear of God' " (52). This is, in the final analysis, the essence of the protagonist, the source of the graceless characterization we mentioned earlier. For Morúa has given us essentially the external dramatization of the young woman, her sad situation, without succeeding in the full expression of her individuality. It is as if the author assumed the view of her that the other characters have, that of the resigned and well-behaved slave, and thus was prevented from discovering the essence that must be hidden beneath her outward appearance. The illegitimate daughter of Don Sebastián de Unzúazo, founder of an illustrious Matanzas family, and of Doña Manuela Corrales, a woman of ill repute who runs several houses of prostitution (239), Sofía seems to have received her dark skin from her mother, a native of the Canary Islands. Abandoned by her mother, she has been raised in the midst of her paternal family as one more of the slaves in service in the house, especially after the premature death of her father. No one knows her origin, nor is there any document to show that she is a slave. As a child, she has suffered the terrible experience of the sugar mill, and this keeps her in a state of constant terror (31).

When the story begins, she is around twenty and, as we have seen, is at the height of her feminine beauty. Therefore, as in the traditional antislavery novel, she is a constant temptation to Fico Unzúazo, the dissipated playboy of the wealthy family. It is clear that we have here a conflict similar to that found in some of the abolitionist stories: the mulatto girl besieged by the eroticism of her own brother. Sofía marshals her moral standards against this passionate siege, even though she loves the young man. She never accepts the invitations she continually receives to take part in the bachitas— licentious entertainments behind closed doors—attended by the young criollos and the prettiest mulatto girls in town (13), and she resists heroically her half-brother's lewd propositions (66). But Sofía thinks she is a mulatto and, as such, she wants to better her social status; she knows the only way of succeeding in that is to unite with a white, in a relation more or less accepted in the system in which it has been her lot to live. Thus, there is a conflict in her mind between the morality learned from Magdalena and her great desire to rise in the ranks of Cuban society: "She suffered a conflict between her modesty, which rebelled at such moral degradation, and her desire to overcome the humiliating social situation that was annihilating her. Who could say that among all the wealthy youths who came to those parties, she could not find someone to liberate her?" (18).

Morúa Delgado places his protagonist in the typical dilemma of the mulatto woman: she must choose either moral degradation or a life without any hope of progressing within the organization that oppresses her. The author's intention here is obviously to emphasize the social, not the ethnic, basis of the practice of concubinage among black and mulatto woman. Sofía, a young white woman, has no other means of forging herself a better situation and a more secure future. Thus, the protagonist shows an elementary class consciousness based on the difference she notices between her and her masters: "white woman are indeed happy . . . they can marry . . . they have their husbands . . . they have servants . . . they are wealthy . . . they can have all the fun they feel like . . . while we . . . I know too well I'll always be the same . . . a poor, miserable slave" (66). The character senses that she is the prisoner of a social determinism that conditions even the least of her acts. This social determinism, which is the thesis of the novel, is based on the nature of slavery, which denies the slaves freedom to direct their lives: "This is how the time passed, apparently prosperous for Sofía; but 'it was written' that the ill-fated girl was never to enjoy real tranquillity. Very logical. Could a slave have any hope for tranquillity?" (53). The plot is based on the fulfillment of that destiny, which in the case of the female slave, like Sofía, will depend on the unbridled eroticism of the slave master. Accordingly, Federico Unzúazo will be the motive force in the tragic experience of seduction, abandonment, shame, and death that constitutes the life of the woman in servitude.

Sofía's life is conceived on a typical *via crucis,* a conception that tends to deprive the character of a dimension of individuality. Here again, the slave experiences disillusionment, but there is no analysis by the author of the repercussions such incidents have on her spirit.

The writer appears to be more attentive to the representational aspect of these occurrences, seen as symptoms of slave society, than to the personal and human values they show in the character. It is indeed true that Sofía feels a kind of love toward Federico, with its related elemental jealousies caused by the other "little mulatto girls" (21)—a love with an admixture of "instinctive fear" (55)—but when she is dishonored by the licentious heir, she gives herself up to the sacrifice with complete passivity. Such an attitude is inexplicable, at least in the domain of her psyche: "Federico drew her to him, and in a lewd rapture, pressed her in his arms with nervous force; and the young woman had neither the wits nor the strength to do anything but give up her body and lay her head on that perfidious chest" (72).

Her dishonor becomes evident in her pregnancy, a physiological phenomenon that gives Morúa Delgado an opportunity to exhibit the medical description for which the naturalists showed such a proclivity. The author uses to the utmost the scientific rhetoric characteristic of the writers of that type of novel. Sofía "could not stand the heaviness and sleepiness that constantly overcame her," "she did not eat, or she ate very little," "she had no desire for anything," and in general she showed all the physical and psychological symptoms of gestation (137). This descriptive technique comes to its climax in the diagnosis and the description of the abortion that Doctor Alvarado has to perform on the girl: "the fetus has lost its normal position; the placenta has come loose and is moving from one side to the other side of the womb, according to the patient's movements; the baby surely has died, and this girl must abort, but immediately; we must not await the slow natural process" (218).

Thus, the incestuous relationship, one of the thematic elements of the abolitionist novel, receives in Sofía a treatment that purports to be objective and naturalistic. The same can be said of the denouement. The young woman dies as a result of the operation, performed too late, and her origins are revealed when her mother claims the anonymous bequest that Sebastián Unzúazo has left to the girl (239).

The determinism of the environment, with which the naturalist novel is nurtured, offers Morúa Delgado the possibility of posing the problem of the blacks in a narrative form based on a positivistic, antilyrical, and objective view of the forces that condition them in the social environment. Except for the differences of technique and period, the attitude of the black novelist we are discussing coincides with the attitude we have observed in the slave Juan Francisco Manzano. In the *Apuntes autobiográficos* and in *Sofía,* it was considered useless and in the long run counterproductive to insist on differentiating ethnic features, whether physical or cultural. What characterizes the slaves is not their blackness but the servitude they must submit to. Once this servitude is legally overcome, the blacks, by means of education, will rise to the same level as the whites and, like the whites, will find themselves able to face the intellectual and civic tasks of the new nation that is being organized. Therefore, in Morúa as in Manzano, there is a desire to become integrated into Cuban life, to be Cuban, without any further adjectival or ethnic classification. This is the idea underlying the writing of a novel about the unusual, although not improbable, case of a white character who finds herself forced to behave like a black. Once the tyranny of slavery ceases, "the emancipated class will stand beside the emancipating class, and in the end all will share equally the deficiencies and perfections that have been produced in the organic forging of their common development" (119).

As we have seen, the characterization of the black protagonist in the Cuban novel of the end of the nineteenth century is based on the same social consciousness we found in the romantic novelists. But this characterization is, in general, sharper, richer, and deeper. The aestheticizing attitude of the last quarter of the century makes it possible to appreciate, as in the case of Zambrana, the authentic beauty of the black, considered in itself and not as a transposition of white beauty. Meza narrates objectively and, for that reason, with a greater will to understand from within the being that has the principal role in his works. Although he did not fully succeed in creating authentic black characters, his protagonists surpass the elementary or "schoolish" image given us by the romantic novelists.

Chapter Six

**The Twentieth Century: Criollismo
and the Avant-Garde**

We can define two generations in the first fifty years of the
Republic in Cuba. The first is made up of those born around 1880;
Félix Lizaso and Raimundo Lazo clearly distinguish two groups
within that generation.[1] In the first group, "lyricism, admiration for
their immediate predecessors, a taste for oratory, and a fondness for
the heroic national theme predominate; in the second, there is a
tendency toward criticism, greater sobriety, and a cosmopolitan tone,
without the disadvantage of the Americanist sentiments of the happy
days of *arielismo,* when optimism could be cultivated without much
effort.[2] José Antonio Ramos (1885–1946), whose novel *Caniquí* (1936)
we shall study in this chapter, is a member of the first group, but
this is a case of generational deviation; he belongs "with the later
groups, much more severe and radical in the carrying out of their
proposals." [3]

The writers who make up the second generation of the Republic
are those born "from the beginning of the last decade of the century
until around the time of the first world war." [4] They are distinguished
by their nonconformity and their innovative zeal in all areas, as they
reacted against the official, rigid, academic standards of the past.
One of their forms of "rebellion" was precisely the revival of the
black theme. This generation has undertaken to surpass the old realism and to secure the triumph of avant-garde literature:

With the founding of the *Revista de avance* in 1927, it found
an adequate vehicle: avant-gardism was to change noticeably

the course of official and academic literature. At the same time
. . . the youth was to participate actively in the resolution of the
serious national problems, and the intellectuals and writers were
gradually to become incorporated into the efforts directed
toward reforming and cleansing public life in Cuba.[5]

It is to this generation, known for its social and literary innovation,
that Alejo Carpentier (1904–) and Lino Novás Calvo (1906–) belong.
The latter, in spite of his Spanish birth, has since childhood been
identified with Cuban life, and it was in Cuba that his literary development took place. Félix Soloni (1900–68) is another member of
this second generation of the Republic; because he was attracted to
the past, he exemplifies a position contrary to that of José Antonio
Ramos.

Besides establishing these Cuban generations, which correspond to
the postmodernist and avant-gardist generations established by José
Juan Arrom,[6] we should mention, for further clarification of the state
of Cuban letters at the beginning of the twentieth century, the paucity
of literary production during the early years of the Republic. As
Salvador Bueno has shown, this crisis was very acute in the narrative
genre. Bueno cites Alejo Carpentier's novel, ¡Ecue-Yamba-O! (1933),
published well into the century, as the Republic's first important
example of the black novel.[7] Even so, a study of the characterization
of the black protagonist by a typical criollista such as Félix Soloni
will give us a better understanding of the new dimensions achieved
in the later narrative.

I   Félix Soloni: Mersé

Félix Soloni (1900–68) in his novel Mersé (1924) establishes the image
of the mulatto woman on the basis of a concept of novelization
that is a sort of dilute and naive naturalism, seasoned with tasty and
picturesque touches from life in Havana in the twenties (life in a
tenement, a superficial view of popular superstitions, and the songs
and dances of the period). This is the story of a mulatto woman who,
conscious of her ethnic situation, wants to escape the "fatal destiny"
the author feels must fall to every mulatto woman. Mersé will fail
in her desire to be a "señorita," apparently because of the designs

of a society that sees this class of women only as instruments of sexual pleasure for men. But the story, laudable in itself as representative of a problem of Cuban society, loses its testimonial value and its literary value due to its simplistic and melodramatic treatment. Social forces cease to be social forces when they become no more than the caprices of the characters who belong to the plutocracy of Havana; these forces are not felt outside these characters, prisoners themselves of the system they think they direct. In addition, there is inconsistency in the development of the plot, due in large part to the rigid archetypes of the characters and to a lack of common sense in its organization. Nevertheless, we find in *Mersé* a "negroism" that shows awareness of the winsome qualities so important in the mulatto, which are well expressed, at least superficially. In the nineteenth-century novel, whites and blacks were united sexually, but it was hard to find any authentic psychic and cultural integration between the races. In *Mersé*, on the contrary, by means of certain folkloric and religious manifestations, we find ourselves in the "gray" area, the predominant segment of the Cuban population. There is an inflection in this novel that—leaving aside the question of literary quality—would be found again in the most representative of those who cultivated the Afro-Antillean poetic movement about to flourish.

Mersé's desire to be a "señorita" is a product of the education she has received from her mother Candelaria. This woman, a rather dark mulatto, is an authentic Catholic, the widow of a soldier who died in a military uprising.[8] She has been a servant for the wealthy Zarzas family, who "loved her and considered her a member of the family," and her daughter was raised with the Zarzas children (7). Mersé has been educated in a nuns' school devoted to the teaching of black children, and the two women live from their work as embroiderers and seamstresses (7). They live in a neighborhood house, a tenement called La Estrella, where their manners and habits are unusual. This exceptional behavior is emphasized by the parallel established with Soledad and her daughters, who are the sister and nieces of Doña Candelaria. To "Chole" (Soledad), it is impossible for the mulatto woman to escape her tragic destiny in Cuban society. Thus, she comments to "Candita": "A mulatto woman cannot be anything but that: a mulatto woman! If she gets refined, the whites look at her askance, even if they are crazy about her, and her own people disdain her, too. If she allows herself to run with the tide, she can as easily become a great lady as a poor unfortunate one. But by no means let her think about marriage!" (10).

Against this idea, Mercedes Leandro (Mersé) will react; in her, to point up the conflict more clearly, we see the dualism between body and spirit that we saw in Antonio Zambrana's Camila. Mersé, although she seems in her mentality and conduct to be almost hypocritically pious, is physically "the prettiest girl in the house," according to the remarks of the Chinese secondhand peddler (12). Thus, her beauty bears the stamp of the topical: she is "the beautiful mulatto girl with all the attractive personality of a twenty-year-old with splendid ways and a passionate racial fieriness" (89). This magnificent body will make her more and more aware of the destiny inherent in the status of the mulatto woman, the destiny her Aunt Chole keeps telling her about. Moreover, the flattery she receives constantly reminds her of her situation; "out in the street they called her 'tasty' and 'sexy'" (28). She will not be able to escape such insolence (13).

Mersé's defense against the society that degrades her is to isolate herself, almost instinctively, from the system. Her life in the neighborhood house is ample proof of the defensive attitude she adopts: "by not going out to the patio to cook, by asking no favors, by not speaking with anyone, she remained on the periphery of the life of the tenement, and by isolating herself, she elevated herself, and there was something inherently superior in her separation from the others" (6). This attitude of distance and differentiation is reflected even in the room the women live in—"one would say it had been brought from some other place" (6)—where the young girl passes her time embroidering or reading. Her library is a picturesque confusion— The Imitation of Christ, María, Fabiola, Creole Cooking—but of all these volumes, her great favorite is the romantic novel by Jorge Isaacs: "María was the one she liked best, and in her twenty-year-old imagination she dreamed of Efraím, loving and handsome, who would some day take her to the altar. This was all that her magnificent youth, the youth of a pretty and beautiful mulatto woman, knew about life and love" (7).

Here the dichotomy between body and spirit is evident. Mersé's idealized view of life is not compatible with the function to which her excellent body condemns her. This body and her status as a mulatto are the determining features of the social characterization to which she must succumb. As Petronila, a negrita prostitute who lives in the tenement, says, "What is the good of this air of superiority she gives herself? After all, she is a mulatto like anyone else, and you'll see, time won't give me the lie: those dead mosquitoes are the ones who do the wildest things" (3).

This air of superiority—"always so serious, so modest, so like a señorita" (165)—shows itself in her relations with her Aunt Soledad and her cousins Crescencia and Charo (Rosario), especially after her mother's death. She cannot bear the life she leads with them, and so, when she finds a relatively secure job, she decides not to go back to her relatives' house (182–83). One of the areas of greatest friction is the difference in religious practices. Like Doña Candelaria, Mersé is a "Mass and Communion" Catholic, who even belongs to parish congregations. The aunt and cousins, on the contrary, have a confused mass of ideas in their heads, preferring communication with "beings" and various ways of predicting the future.

It is precisely in the practice of these rites that Mersé's destiny is revealed, apparently in sibylline form. The cataleptic trance of Orosia —a sort of medium in the "seances" celebrated by the aunt and cousins—proclaims the intense racial hatred that is developing in the protagonist's psyche. When the congregation meets around the "spiritual water" and the spirit of the Indian Alí is "concretized," Alí pronounces, through the mouth of the celebrant: "She is a spirit which has not yet, in this incarnation, opened her loving soul, but who in other incarnations loved much and therefore is condemned to hate much in this one" (23). This destiny of hate, according to another prediction of the spirit of Alí, will be accomplished when Mersé's "hour comes" (130). These spiritist revelations will be consummated by the "warning" seen in the "four inverted aces," which appear by chance when Anita "throws cards" for Mersé; the way the cards fall signifies betrayal and dishonor (178–79). We should note here that the superficial treatment of these practices and the purely enunciative function they have in the story hinder the creation of an atmosphere in which fantasy and reality might be joined and become almost interchangeable terms. We are not faced here with a magical view of reality, because what the author perceives as real always dominates and shapes the world of myth and superstition. There is no penetration of that world, only a kind of coloristic and picturesque description of it, used to introduce a motive for the denouement of the novel.

For this reason, these practices do not illuminate the ultimate being of the protagonist; they are simply indications of her future, of what "will happen to her." The discomfort she feels after the first seance is a result of her feelings of uncertainty about the future, that is, the combination of outside forces that can enter into her existence. There is no confrontation with her authentic, essential being; what develops in Mersé is, rather, a tendency to dream and worry about her possibilities:

> She had said nothing to her mother about what had happened at Soledad's house; but on account of the secrecy she was guarding, the scene in which she had been almost the protagonist took on the greatest importance in her mind. They had said that she would love much. And whom was she going to love? She knew no one. Would she finally meet her Beloved? A proud smile passed over her lips. [25]

The accomplishment of her "most cruel destiny" (189) is the result of her relationship with Cuca Zarzas and Ernesto Valeto, playgirl and playboy of Havana society, both old friends with whom she had played childhood games. The protagonist silently loves Ernesto, and thus an amorous triangle is developed, which is complicated by the presence of Aristarco Pérez, Cuca's husband. The mulatto girl will be forced to act as a go-between for the "white señorita" and the man who deeply attracts her. The embroidery and couturier shop founded by the sisterhood of Las Damas Piadosas (the Pious Ladies), whose directorship was entrusted to Mersé, is the place chosen for the meeting between Cuca and Ernesto (148). But the adultery never takes place; when Mersé discovers that Aristarco knows about the plan and is preparing a scandal with a view to bringing suit for divorce, she takes Cuca's place. When the judicial functionaries appear in the shop, they find the mulatto girl "submitting" to Ernesto (204). But if the great social scandal does not take place, Mersé's generous act brings about her public dishonor and consequently the loss of her job (224). Abandoned by Cuca and even by Ernesto, whose mistress she does not care to become, she must lose all hope of becoming señorita Mercedes Leandro. The only thing she can aspire to is being a "mulatto bitch" (212).

This difficult experience develops an awareness of class and race in the protagonist. For this reason, when she finds herself obliged to be a go-between, she says to one of the workmen in the shop: "It is the tiresome business of gratitude.... The rich give ... what is left over, as an affectation, out of convention, or for sport ... and then, when they ask for something, when they remind you of what they've given ... they compromise and endanger those they have protected" (202). Later, when she has been completely abandoned, we see surging in Mersé "all the ancestral rebelliousness of an oppressed race" (219), which allows her to confront Cuca and scold her severely: "When we (just as much women as you) love, then they say we have lovers! When you do the same thing they say you are flirting! ... I have a lover! How I wish I had him! After all it isn't very hard, especially if you are a 'playgirl'! There is so little woman in you people!" (219).

Socially, therefore, Mercedes is the typical mulatto woman; appearances force her to be Ernesto's mistress. Her tragedy is in having tried to be different when a whole system, based on prejudice, marks the mulatto pejoratively from birth. As the narrator says: "She was a piece of the immense social timepiece which insisted on turning in the opposite direction from the way it was supposed to, and as a consequence, all the gears that operated it were impaired, stopped working, and made it fly in pieces" (237).

The obvious determinism that fills this citation, but which the author did not succeed in bringing fully into the novel due to the superficial way the motives of the plot are strung together, is supposed to be the explanation of the intense hatred and the desire for revenge that Mersé experiences. Accordingly, the fullest realization of the mulatto being of the protagonist comes to be the oft-repeated, typical image of the magnificent mulatto woman, full of bottled-up jealousies and vengeance, following the abandonment that has victimized her. Mercedes Leandro is the new version of Cecilia Valdés, dressed here in the slightly coarser taste of the twenties. Soloni has arrived at the same result as Villaverde, although by a different route. Thus, Mersé, assimiliated to the gay life of her cousins, becomes the "queen of the balls" (246). One of these events gives her the opportunity to carry out her plan of revenge: to lead Aristarco, "perfectly drunk," to Cuca's feet. The humiliation felt by Cuca satisfies the mulatto girl's wounded pride. Her destiny as a mulatto fulfilled, "condemned always to fall or to make fall," Mersé dies of an accidental overdose of medicine taken upon her return to the party (250). As the dying girl is being taken to the hospital, the musicians, unaware of what has happened, are playing, in honor of the "queen of the ball," the famous *son:*

> Some say at one o'clock.
> And others say at three.
> Ay! Witchery, witchery!
> Witchery killed Mersé!
> [251]

A study of the characterizaton of the mulatto woman in this novel shows a concept of the woman and the social environment she faces that reflects a typical and superficial attitude. A story that seeks to impress with the recourses of melodrama, serial writing, and a certain demogoguery, it is illustrative of the stereotype of the black that later writers concerned with the black character had to confront and surpass. Félix Soloni follows the old formula of giving us the mulatto character in the cold light of the picturesque, creating a whole in which each detail has the purpose of documenting the local color found in the elements of a romantic engraving. In this way, he achieves a rarefied atmosphere, at once of a museum and of a farce, which leaves the bitter aftertaste of old age without dignity.

II   Lino Novás Calvo: *El negrero*

If, as we have seen, *Mersé* was a clear example of the ethical and aesthetic rigidity and naiveté that generally prevailed in the Cuban novel before the appearance of avant-garde literature, *El negrero* (1933) by Lino Novás Calvo (1905–), because of its conscious desire for narrative innovation, illustrates the stamp of renewal that characterizes the new literature. This is clear in the efforts of Novás Calvo to create an essentially objective novelistic world, which owes nothing to worn-out nineteenth-century realism or to the traditional Spanish-American *criollismo*. Novás's technique is what stands out most clearly in this "novelized life" of Pedro Blanco Fernández de Trava, one of the biggest slave traders of the first decades of the nineteenth century. We could define this technique as "essential realism," according to the definition given by Enrique Anderson-Imbert and Lawrence B. Kiddle:

> Novás Calvo does not add imaginative touches to reality; on the contrary, one would say that he reduces reality to its elemental outlines. However, he cannot be called a realist because the retarded movements of his characters, the suggestive power of their gestures, words, and even expressive silences, and the constant interruptions in the continuity of the story startle the reader and force him to contribute imaginatively to what he is reading.[9]

This reduction of reality to its elemental lines brings with it a sort of cinematographic expression. As José Antonio Portuondo has shown, Lino Novás's narrative fiction relates the peripetias in the lives of his characters "with a technique that is somewhat cinematographic in the way it suggests emotions without describing them, simply by presenting successive situations that lead the reader gradually to the desired emotional state."[10] The author himself corroborates the opinion of these critics when he explains in a few words his own concept of style and narrative technique; he sought "the objective narration of facts. . . . And I could not find it. At that time nobody knew how to narrate objectively. Everyone felt subjective and lyrical."[11] This antilyrical attitude seems to come from his reading of contemporary American and English novelists. José Antonio Portuondo and Salvador Bueno have found traces of Caldwell, Steinbeck, Faulkner, and Hemingway, as well as of James Joyce, D. H. Lawrence, and Aldous Huxley, of whom Novás was an excellent translator.[12] For this reason, "he represents a new development in the history of the Spanish-American short story."[13]

¡Ecue-Yamba-O! by Alejo Carpentier and El negrero constitute the best novelistic expression achieved by the Cuban negroist movement of the thirties.[14] Although Novás Calvo's story has no black protagonist, mention of it is indispensable in this study because it is the black viewed in the aggregate that shapes the adventurous life of Pedro Blanco, as well as the lives of all the professionals in the slave trade who appear in the novel. To re-create these lives, Novás consulted an impressive bibliography, but "none of that vast erudition had discharged its aridities onto the story. In a sparkling and terse

style, full of movement, the adventures follow one another, convey-
ing a wealth of emotions." [15]

In Novás Calvo's novel, the black is perceived as a collective character, against whom the protagonist Pedro Blanco stands out. But
this background, apparently amorphous, has an effect that transforms
the spirit of the trader. The destiny of these merchants in human flesh
is illustrated metaphorically: "the soul of the slave trader was as
black as the Negro" (62), a fact that, in the case of Pedro, makes for
a sort of mulatto state of mind, with the dual resentment usually
present in people of mixed breeding. "All the trade in Negroes was
the work of mulattoes, (whether in the color of their skin, or in the
color of their spirit). And Pedro was a mulatto inside" (221). In fact,
the protagonist's establishment in Africa is a miniature imitation of
a European court, in whose decoration the assimilation of African
aesthetic elements is apparent.

A basic source of interest in the story is the objective view of the
slave trade and of slavery. There is no discernible individualization
of the black, but the miserable commerce in their own flesh that
these people have to suffer brings with it an aggregating image of
the race. In addition, we can see how the most relevant facts of such
a sad enterprise deeply mark the character of Pedro Blanco, which
suggests the interchange of influences already mentioned. In the last
analysis however, these manifestations of the slave trade stand out
not only for their documentary and historical value but also in their
capacity for suggesting the essential ethnic features of people in such
a dramatic conjuncture. What we want to point out here are the racial
features of a collective personage that underly this story and give it a
very peculiar human touch.

In this objective view of the slave trade, we witness the process
of "civilization" to which a race is condemned, from the time of its
capture in the jungles to its sale and exploitation in the markets of
America. The caravan of slaves that winds through the interior of the
African continent toward the coast shows, in addition to the rebelliousness of the blacks, their rhythmic and musical instinct, as well
as their attachment to family and tribe (81). The description of a
slave ship, which enumerates all its torturesome details and peculiar-
ities, has its ultimate value in re-creating the spirit that animates it,
embodied in the "Negro plague." This plague causes "every man that
enlists in it to acquire the soul of a Negro immediately" (44). A

crossing in one of these ships is perceived as a test of strength in the face of mutual human cruelty and the rigors of nature. On his first trip, Pedro notices that "from the hold of the ship there came a dead sound, as if the voices had no escape, as if someone were talking behind a glass" (83). The sound comes from the blacks who are making the crossing, heaped together in suffocating proximity and suffering from lack of water and ventilation. The dead and dying are thrown indiscriminately into the sea, the drinking water is contaminated, the rations become scarce, and the ship is detained by the great tropical calms of the South Atlantic. Delirium threatens, and once again only music can raise the spirits of the black horde: "the guards got out the drum. . . . The whip went with it. The Negroes began to dance heavily" (85). Again, it is the African rhythms that facilitate the disembarkation of the "cargo" in the ports of the New World (63). It is as if, by imposing an ancestral rhythm on the Africans, the slave trader were taking possession of their souls.

At a slave market in Recife, the protagonist reveals the contradiction in the depths of his being—one of Novás's greatest successes. On the one hand, Pedro's imagination is strongly attracted by the dealer and his typical garb; on the other hand, we note his complete insensitivity to the moral degradation inherent in the auctioning of human flesh. Thus, Pedro's imagination converts the trader, who makes the slaves dance to the terrible sound of the whip, into a sort of pirate captain, "playing the guitar or commanding a horde of vagabonds" (65). But he is also attracted by the riches obtained from this trade: "Pedro wasn't concerned with that"—the suffering of the black man from the stocks, the whip, and the branding irons of slavery. The plight of the blacks awakens in him only the desire for power and wealth, canceling in his mind the sentimental tendencies we had noted in his childhood in Málaga (66). It is the primitivism with which the black is treated, as well as the complete dependency and defenselessness of the slave in relation to the traders, that causes Pedro's descent to an infrahuman state, marking his spirit definitively. As he sees how the overseer "sounded the whip, and made the captives dance, talk, sing, run, and laugh" (66), Pedro comes to form a concept of human life in which only force, cruelty, and astuteness seem to be effective. As in the abolitionist novel of the nineteenth century, in El negrero slavery perverts the white man by making him a slave to his lowest passions and his self-concern.

Novás develops this theme with particular success in the episode in the Cuban sugar mill. Pedro has been made administrator of a sugar plantation, and, in complicity with other white employees and some black ones, he wants to incite the workers to rebel for his own personal benefit, a motivation that does not exclude the hatred and resentment he feels toward the owner of the sugar mill and his family. He conceives a plan that takes account of the slightest eventuality, but the plan fails because he has not foreseen the Dionysian state of the blacks when they are involved in ancestral dances. All distinction among the slaves is wiped out, and the slaves the crafty administrator had counted on have been fused with the others, who are dominated by the primitive bellicose instinct of the runaway. Pedro has let loose a force he has no acquaintance with:

> The drums were emitting a long howl like those of cavemen, and everyone (men, women, girls, and boys) had become part of the dance. . . . Pedro had the feeling that something abnormal was occurring there. . . . The suppressed rebelliousness they had in them was beginning to speak to them within, and the tom-tom was replying more and more violently to that magnetic fluid that gripped the group of Negroes. Pedro was now feeling the result. [105]

We see again that it is the rhythm of the ancestral drum that conditions the minds of these people, as Novás conceives them. That rash attempt shows Pedro that "there were secret and treacherous forces capable of transforming and diverting actions" (106), but it also reveals to us the function of the black as a collective personage in *El negrero,* in addition to his characterization as a primitive and atavistic being, deeply incited by rhythm. Accordingly, there is no idealization or lyricism of any sort, only the crude and naked reality of a person subjected to the most terrible kind of servitude.

III   José A. Ramos: *Caniquí*

In contrast to the effort of Novás Calvo to write a novel that objectifies the collective personality of the black, in *Caniquí* (1936) by José A. Ramos (1885–1946) the characterization of the black protagonist corresponds to the symbolic function assigned to him. Caniquí, a black slave, is in the last analysis the symbol of Cuba; his individual destiny is conceived as an expression of the stages of development of the Cuban people. The novel, apparently a historical reconstruction, is in fact an examination of the essence of Cuban nationality in an attempt to understand its present and its future. In this "eternal valley of Trinidad, past and future are confused," as they also are in the pages of the story.[16] The novelization of Trinidad life between 1830 and 1833 is a point of departure for arriving at the essence and the potential of Cuban society. Juan J. Remos y Rubio points out that "the political thesis in this novel is based on historical sources, and it has as the scene of its drama the traditional city of Trinidad, the best atmosphere for evocation and contrasts." [17] *Caniquí* is the result of a slow gestation period, coinciding with the political and economic crisis suffered by Cuba between 1928 and 1935. In this novelistic invention, imagination and history are integrated, following the illustrative purpose mentioned above. The story leads to an understanding of the Cuban problem, which comes to be the most valuable substance of the work and at the same time its reason for being. José Antonio Ramos felt that his desire to use the novel to shed light on the true nature of his people at a critical moment in their history might be the basis of a scandal, or worse still, of a conspiracy of silence that could impede a real understanding of his book. In the prologue, he says, "*Caniquí* will not be read with respect, nor will it be understood in my country, who knows for how many years? Consequently, its publication is far from being its last vicissitude. Perhaps my book will awaken some interest in other intellectual centers of Spanish America or in North American university circles, a noble community that has nothing to do with Wall Street and does not approve of its country's role in our Columbian land" (7–8). This conception of the novel reflects, as Portuondo has said, "a new point of view, more true to reality" in Ramos, that brings him to "an immersion in the past in search of the roots of Cuban nationality in the nineteenth century. . . . from that plunge into the past he returned bringing renewed faith and enthusiasm and the best of his novels: *Caniquí*." [18] Thus, the characterization of the black protagonist in this novel is a product of Ramos's understanding of Cuba's historic past. For this reason, we must focus in this study on Filomeno Bicunía Caniquí from two points of view: as a character in fiction and as a mythical symbol.

Ramos's originality lies in his having broken with the stigmatized legendary view, now found in the folklore of the Cuban people, of this Trinidadian bandit of the first decades of the nineteenth century. The popular expression, "You are more evil than Caniquí" changes its connotation and is enriched with new meanings when the personality of the hero is re-created in the story as a counterpoint to the social context in which it develops. As the figure of this fugitive black is contrasted with the characteristics of the white society, Caniquí acquires a revolutionary dimension. But Ramos's greatest accomplishment is having left the black in his essential state, without additions that would change his authentic profile. Caniquí's symbolic value issues naturally from his actions and his feelings; he is a symbol, but he does not know he is. There is no preachment on his part; the insensitive "cimarron" is limited simply to living. But this is because in Ramos's opinion one possible danger for his country is also that it might "hide in a *palenque*" (forest refuge for runaways). In this way, personal fate and national fate are parallel, the first being a prototype of the second.

Filomeno Bicunía is the historical source of the legend of Caniquí, who belonged to the collection of slaves held by Don Lorenzo de Pablos. In his first appearance in the story, the instinct for liberty that is the most characteristic mark of his nature is brought out. The overseers who have just caught the runaway are bringing him before the "master":

> The prisoner had thrown himself calmly to the ground like a tired animal. He was resting his head facedown on the ground on his outstretched arms. His wrists were tied with a coarse rope. . . . His sparse clothing, torn into grimy pieces, left uncovered his tremendous torso, lumpy with muscles, covered with earth, and of a color that could not be discerned in the deepening twilight. [61–62]

But the principal function of this objective and external description is to indicate the protagonist's physical presence; the deeper characterization will be inferred from the reactions of the master and from the attitude adopted by his daughter and her fiancé, Juan Antonio. The slave, who in the abolitionist novel was reduced to a passive object, becomes in Ramos's story the cause of reactions in the other characters. Caniquí, to a large extent, changes the conduct of the whites, especially of the young couple.

At the sight of the poor black man Don Lorenzo reviews the slave's history. In this way we learn how he came into the hands of the wealthy *hacendado;* we learn about his relationship with Lorencito, the now-dead heir of the landowner, and about his ethnic background: "But Filomeno was not bad. He was a mischievous little Negro. Ma Irene insisted he was her great-grandson and that he had some Chinese in him. With poor little Lorencito, his son—may God keep him in his holy grace—he had been like a dog: good and faithful" (62).

But the author moves rapidly beyond these anecdotal details to enter fully into the marrow of his character: Caniquí's individuality. Don Lorenzo, in a fit of anger more apparent than real, repentant liberal that he is, allows the admiration he feels for the slave to slip through—an admiration that stems from the primitive sense of freedom shown by the black man. This feeling is so deeply rooted in the spirit of the slave that it overcomes any other consideration: "The day he fled toward the forest he had announced it to the master. . . . 'Tie me up, master, or put me into the stocks!' Don Lorenzo repeated the slave's words as he remembered them, adding an absurd emphasis, in his state of confusion, 'or else I'll run away!' " (62–63).

Mariceli and her fiancé are deeply influenced by the graphic expression of the slave. In Juan Antonio the teachings of his Professor Saco are transformed into a total way of life, and in this character an evolution begins from a theoretical liberalism to revolutionary practice (63). Mariceli is a child very much influenced by religious beliefs, and when she compared Caniquí's situation with that of Jesus, she "experienced a strange shaking, from identification with the slave. She wanted to feel his fatigue, his pain, his tortures. And to be strong like him!" (64). What has begun as a religious experience is transformed into a basically human attitude, cleansed of the false and sickly mysticism to which the suffocating provincial life had inclined the girl. The slave, without realizing it, has started the young couple on the road to liberation from the dark forces that possess them.

Caniquí's smile, a mixture of defiance and a sense of the enjoyment of existence, which persists in the protagonist throughout the narration, is a key to penetrating his psychology and the meaning of the novel. The slave laughs proudly, for example, when Don Lorenzo repeats his words (63) or when Don Lorenzo visits him while he is in the stocks—in both cases, significantly, raising his head: "The slave, with a violent contortion that made the stocks creak, managed to raise his head. And between his thick lips, smeared with corn, there again appeared the double row of teeth, in the eternal smile" (80). The black slave, facing the "master," senses his own value, the invincible nature of his atavistic rebellion, and, at the same time, the insubstantial and perishable nature of an authority more apparent than real. This is the pleasure that Caniquí experiences: knowing that he is stronger, even at the moment of death (300). Moreover, this pleasure is not diminished by the knowledge of his own destiny: " 'Caniquí, you bad Negro, you're going to die by hanging!' he was repeating. . . . It was a song of grandmother Ma Irene with which he habitually expressed, in his way, his unworried and virile acceptance of Destiny" (107).

These are the fundamental characteristics that influence the white characters, especially Mariceli and Juan Antonio, whose reactions, products of the black man's example, also characterize the slave. In the face of that significant smile, Mariceli identifies with Caniquí: "she felt like laughing, too, and enjoying the triumph of the unhappy slave over the powerful and wrathful father" (64). As for the young lawyer, when he remembers the slave's words, "Tie me up, because if you don't I shall run away," he senses that, "confronted by the rebelliousness of the Negro, they . . . both felt in harmony. In Caniquí he was to find the courage to confront the Master. And she, too, was the victim of that malicious, despotic, and brutal power that played with their lives" (290). For Mariceli and Juan Antonio, too, feel like slaves. Don Lorenzo treats the young girl like one of his marriageable slaves; he speaks of the young man as if he were a bull or a horse, and what interests him is that they have, like the slaves, good progeny, who naturally are to be males. "And no females. If the first birth was a female, a *chancleta* [an old slipper, a Cuban synechdochic term for a black female], he himself would throw her into the well head first. Males, every one, she should give birth to" (42). Thus, the couple is reduced to an infrahuman level, the level of cattle. Mariceli, aware of this, will refuse the love of her cousin and give herself over to the excesses of misguided mysticism. The young lawyer will bungle his way through the confused requirements of his profession.

To liberate themselves, they will find an example and strength in Caniquí. The slave is the inspiration that extricates them from the terrible circumstances in which they find themselves. We could say that the black's lesson is learned by the whites. The slave has never been able to comprehend the hatred, the inhibitions, and the distrust of his masters, and for this reason Caniquí feels the pointlessness of the mortifications Mariceli imposes on herself in a moment of exalted asceticism. When he keeps the girl from carrying to its logical end the penitence with which she is flagellating herself, he advises her: "The young lady should not pay any attention when they tell her Caniquí is bad. The people are worse than Caniquí. They say that the young lady is bad, too, very bad. But I know it isn't so. The young lady should not live in Trinidad, young lady. Go far away! Tell the Master to take you away. Or Juan Antonio, the young man" (292).

Indeed, in the society of the whites there is no place for love—only for slander, fear, and exploitation. Juan Antonio, standing before Caniquí's body, which has been exposed in the public square, comes to understand this society and rejects it; he also comes to understand the deep being of Mariceli, also a victim of the deformation of that system he now condemns. For "Caniquí, still and destroyed, had spoken to him in a miracle. At once all his doubts were resolved!" (307). Thus it is that they escape together from the accursed provincial city, consummating the passion that unites them out in the world of nature, which at that moment takes on a symbolic dimension (314). Because of the slave, the young couple has overcome the material and spiritual servility that subjugated them.

The basic characterological procedure used by Ramos is the development of the particular concrete form taken by the African magical-mystical world in the mind of Caniquí. This idea of what is religious begins with a joyful view of nature, in which the slave finds the realm of genuine liberty, which attracts him with an irresistible force. It is the domain of the sea spirit, Olokún, symbol of the full life, which exerts such an attraction on the slave, deeply marking his psychology. But what impels him toward the forest refuge of the runaways with no less intensity is Elegbará, a violent and bloodthirsty god: "The Master had promised to keep his wages for his manumission. Some day he would work at his trade for himself . . . if the forest did not tempt him again with that itch, with that impulse from Elegbará himself, which he had felt since that morning without knowing why" (145). As we see, the slave poses for himself the dilemma of integrating himself into an unjust society or fighting against it in terms of his own religious concept of the world.

To Caniquí, the notions of Christianity he has learned from the lips of the slave Rosario are a superficial cover, under which his firm African beliefs are hidden. These beliefs have been taught him by Ma Irene, his great-grandmother, who is an African black. Consequently, the phenomenon of religious syncretism is produced in his mind, as an original equation is established between the African deities and certain manifestations of the cult and theology of Christianity. For example, God the Father and Christ come to be identified with Obatalá and his infinite power in the thought of the slave (146). But in the last analysis, what counts for Caniquí is the African cosmogony—Birí, god of the night, and Orúmbila, the rising sun, which "in the splendid tropical mornings communicated an intense happiness to his spirit" (147). It is the deification of nature and the animism with which his soul endows all the elements of creation that make him able to feel that harmonious and beautiful universe. Against the white attitude that inhibits the basic natural impulses of the human being, Caniquí forms a concept of man and life that tends to seek the equilibrium between the creative and the destructive forces of the universe. Thus, to Obatalá the slave opposed Elegbará, a demoniac power, which Ramos, with paradoxical intent, converts into a vital force that carries Caniquí into the realm of liberty and the Dionysian, symbolized by Olokún, the sea spirit. The essential point, however, is that the slave, rather than believing—in the Occidental religious sense of the term—feels the presence of these forces experientially. This is an animistic interpretation of the cosmos. Every element in this universe comes to be a deity, and thus, perceiving those elemental forces of which it is composed, Caniquí reverts to the names that symbolize them:

> Among the mysterious concavities of the hills, at last, as in the enormous branches of the old god-tree, in the fire, in the rain, and in the fruits of the earth and in the flowers, which constantly shook his spirit with deep emotions, Filomeno was reluctant to concede that there was no benevolent and protective

spirit, as he had sensed it himself in his earliest childhood, before learning it as part of the traditions of his race. [147]

Thus the traditions of his race eventually corroborate what his spirit has already sensed. Caniquí is a pagan, in the noblest sense of the word. Therefore, geographical and astronomical phenomena take on a sacred meaning for the slave. For example, as he contemplates the dawn, the slave sees that "Birí, overcome, rolled himself into monstrous torsos and heads against the mountains. . . . and on the other side, on the fixed horizon of the water, the magnificient Orúmbila began to hurl into the sky the blood of his agonizing enemy, only to appear again later, calm and serene, in the bright and ever-clearer blue of the sky" (173).

This joyous understanding of and pleasure in nature becomes more acute before the unlimited spectacle of the sea spirit Olokún, whom Caniquí perceives as his own special protector against the malicious power of Elegbará. The latter god "had been savage since his birth, because Calixta had given ear to a man of another race: a Chinese" (148). This explanation of his tragic destiny is resisted and annulled in Caniquí's mind by the surge of freedom he feels when faced with the power of water. His exaltation is what makes him believe firmly in the beneficial influence of the god who rules over rivers, lakes, and seas; Elegbará, "the terrible god, would be unable to do anything against him so long as the spirit Olokún did not permit it," and it is for this reason that Filomeno "did not seek the hideouts of the other runaways, but sought instead the bank of some river, a lake, or the beach" (148). And it is because of that belief that he can be killed. When he realizes he is being pursued, he enters the kingdom of "Olokún, the blessed, a knife in his right hand, and his mouth free to laugh loudly," because "he felt that they could do nothing to him" (299). When they scare him into giving up, "he had the notion of holding his face up, to express himself better: his life was all he saw and enjoyed on that tropical morning. . . . Blue! Magnificent Obatalá! Freedom in the expanses of space: in the air, in the sea! Freedom, fullness . . ." (300). While he is feeling this emotion, he receives his death blow.

It is obvious here that the anecdotal has a symbolic dimension, the ultimate objective of José Antonio Ramos in the characterization of his protagonist. As John E. Englekirk has pointed out, Caniquí "is a symbol of colonial Cuba vacillating between feelings of loyalty to the Master, Spain, and the invincible impulse for liberty." [19] This, then, is the ultimate significance of the black man's words to Don Lorenzo, "Tie me up, my master, for if you don't I shall run away," as well as of the whole life of this hardened runaway and of his intense love of nature and of freedom. When his life is understood by Mariceli and Juan Antonio, Filomeno's being takes on a meaning that achieves the symbolic intent of the writer. It is, at the same time, the novel's message of hope, for the young people are going to relive the fate of the poor slave in their own capacities. This is Juan Antonio's thought when he says to Mariceli: "Caniquí is a symbol. His tremendous energy, his physical vigor, his happiness like that of a young, healthy animal, are not good only for him. Cuba is also a wellspring of wealth, youth, and happiness. But . . . everything she has belongs to her Master, to her possessor" (165). Thus the life of Caniquí indicates to the lawyer what his task as a man should be: securing the freedom his country needs.

This is the core of the novel, the central thought that determines its structure. It was this purpose that José Antonio Ramos followed in the creation of his black protagonist. Without weakening the objective external image, expressed through the character's historical role as the author perceived it, we arrive in a sphere that is beyond the reality of nineteenth-century Cuba and is the source of the unreal episodes narrated. This illumination of the underlying reality is the ultimate sustenance of Cuba, the root of nationality in her crucial formative century. The black Caniquí is the novelistic expression of this critical source. Thus, both the novel and the hero are models for understanding and teaching. This story goes beyond the picturesque, the melodramatic, and the coloristic in the characterization of the black protagonist, bringing us a view of the black man that reflects the desire to illuminate the true character of a nation. Because he probes the very heart of the country and its fondest aspirations, Ramos's ultimate message achieves a dimension of universality: "Caniquí has not died. And may he never die! The people will be afraid again tomorrow. The ghost of this bandit they think has died will be followed by others and still others. . . . And we honorable men shall have to become bandits, too, in order to destroy at once this curse of the White Masters and those servile hordes of slaves" (310).

IV Alejo Carpentier: *¡Ecue-Yamba-O!; El reino de este mundo.*

In the same year that *El negrero* appeared in Madrid, *¡Ecue-Yamba-O!* (1933), "an African story" by Alejo Carpentier (1904–), was also published. With this novel, this Cuban writer initiates novelistic work that is "founded on basic realities, common to all, in the social and philosophical drama of modern man, and conceived within the sphere of authentic American mythology."[20] Indeed, the work of Carpentier, taken as a whole, constitutes one of the most consistent examples in the contempoary Spanish-American novel of overcoming the limitations of the *criollista* technique, which in many cases had succeeded only in giving us the picturesque and superficial in the world it proposed to depict. Carpentier's work is defined as he seeks to interpret the real America and to react against that superficial conception of the novel; but at the same time, because he has learned the lesson of the criollistas and of the European surrealists, he brings to his novels the deep reality of Latin America. In his essay, "Problemática de la actual novela latinoamericana," we find corroboration of this. With reference to criollismo, Carpentier makes the following observation: "the naturalistic-nativistic-typicalist-vernacular method applied for more than thirty years to the writing of novels in Latin America has given us a regional and picturesque novel that has rarely arrived at the depth of things or the really transcendental."[21] This assertion makes very clear the search to which Alejo Carpentier has addressed himself in his creative work.

In order to achieve this objective of depth and universality, the novelist will rid himself of the structural axis of the criollistas— space—and replace it with the idea of time. The importance given by the criollistas to nature in Spanish America is obvious. On the contrary, in Carpentier's work we see that the landscape has been replaced by the notion of becoming, the line on which he constructs his stories. This explains Carpentier's persistence in writing historical novels. In "Confesiones sencillas de un escritor barroco," he declared:

> I'm very fond of historical themes for two reasons: because to me modernity does not exist in the sense usually given that word; man is sometimes the same in different periods, and placing him in his past can be the same as placing him in the present. The second reason is that the novel of love between two or more characters never has interested me.[22]

Thus, the historical novel becomes a means of understanding the permanent essences of man and his inalterable nature throughout time. In addition, while understanding man's past one is at the same time bringing his present to light. Hence, Carpentier's intent goes beyond that of erudite reconstruction of history. The historical events are contemporized in the novel and form a texture into which the destinies of the particular figures are woven, gaining their fundamental meaning and definition. Thus, Alejo Carpentier's historical novel is consistent with the fundamental principal that governs his novelistic work. In his vision of the past, the Cuban author is also penetrating the motive forces of the "praxis" of the contemporary literary environment. This praxis, identified with the Sartrean "contexts" (racial, economic, political, cultural, ideological, and so on), defines the American man through repercussion and echo, a process of "outside-inside." [23] Accordingly, the "brilliance" of the author lies in elucidating the Spanish American through a clarification of the hidden motive forces of the reality in which he finds himself.

A universal expression of the profound relationship between the many aspects of the reality of Latin America might be the formula for explaining the substance of Carpentier's narrative work and the purpose that inspires it. He himself has summarized the process of achieving this purpose, at the same time giving us an overall view of his novelistic work:

> I felt an ardent desire to express American society. I still did not know how. The difficulty of the task was a challenge because of my lack of understanding of American essences. I devoted many long years to reading everything I could about America. For nearly eight years I did almost nothing but read American texts. I think by the end of those years I had formed an idea of what this continent was. I have mentioned that I moved away from surrealism because it seemed to me that it would offer nothing to this continent. But surrealism did mean a lot to me. It taught me to see textures, aspects of American life that I had not noticed, engulfed as we were in the wave of nativism brought by Güiraldes, Gallegos, and José Eustasio Rivera. I understood that behind this nativism there was something more, what I call contexts: a tellurian context and an epicopolitical one; the author who finds the relation between these two will write the American novel.[24]

Very evident from this citation is Carpentier's intent to surpass criollismo, an intent fundamental to his art; equally evident is his debt to
European surrealism. Yet, in the prologue to *El reino de este mundo*
(1949), he attacks "irreverently [the] fantastic code" of the surrealists when he expounds his theory of "marvelous reality." [25] To him,
the entire history of America is a chronicle of marvelous reality, which
he explains as the product of "an unexpected change in reality
(the miracle), of a privileged revelation of reality, of an unusual or
uniquely auspicious illumination of the unknown riches of reality,
of a broadening of the dimensions or kinds of reality, perceived with
particular intensity due to an exaltation of the spirit which leads it
to a sort of 'borderline state.' " In addition, marvelous reality is "the
patrimony of all America, where as yet no inventory of cosmogonies
has been completed. It is found at every step in the lives of the men
who have inscribed dates in the history of the continent and who
have left surnames that carry over into the present." [26]

Having thus clarified the basic elements that make up the novelistic
work of Alejo Carpentier and having placed the work in the context
of Spanish-American novelistic art, we can undertake a study of the
black protagonist in *¡Ecue-Yamba-O!* and in *El reino de este mundo*.
Besides, this study will help to make us aware of the transformation
that the concept and technique of the novel undergo in the Cuban
novelist.

We have seen that Carpentier belongs to the avant-garde generation, the group in Cuba that "discovered" the black and the black
theme.[27] This subject matter can be observed in all segments of
Carpentier's work: ballets (*La rebanbaramba*, 1928, and *El milargro
de Anaquillé*, 1929), novels, short stories ("Viaje a le semilla," 1944),
lyrical work and texts for music ("Poèmes des Antilles," 1929, "La
passion noire," 1932). Furthermore, his critical and investigatory work
has been concerned with the black aspects of Cuban culture, as, for
example in *La música en Cuba* (1946).

The curious phenomenon of the absence of the black theme, which
we had noted in Cuban letters during the early years of independence, is explained to us by Carpentier in his study, "Variaciones
sobre un tema cubano":

A process of rapproachement to the Negro theme was noted,
accentuated by the fact that the writers and artists of the cosmopolitan period had obstinately closed their eyes to the pres-

ence of the Negro on the island, ashamed of it . . . Then, in reaction to this discriminatory spirit, they moved toward the Negro with an enthusiasm that was almost excessive, finding in the Negro ambit certain values preferable to others, perhaps more lyrical, but much less forceful.[28]

The Cuban negroist movement, then, forms part of the reaction of the avant-garde generation to a Republic completely lacking in any substantive or transcendental meaning. In *La música en Cuba*, Carpentier adds that thus was born "the Afro-Cuban tendency, which for more than ten years would nurture poems, novels, and folkloric and sociological studies. It was a tendency that in many cases touched only on the superficial and peripheral . . . but which was a necessary step in understanding certain poetic, musical, ethnic, and social factors that had contributed to giving the indigenous a physiognomy of its own." [29]

¡Ecue-Yamba-O! belongs to the Cuban negroist movement, and even though this movement imposes its limitations on the story, the novel nevertheless constitutes this first necessary step in the author's narrative work toward a better comprehension of the being and situation of the black. Carpentier wrote the original version of the novel in a Havana jail, between the first and ninth of August in 1927 and edited the definitive text in Paris from January to August of 1933.[30] Carpentier duly informs us about the circumstances and the cultural milieu in which the novel took shape:

> They put me in jail in 1927 for signing a manifesto against Machado. . . . In prison I began to write my first novel, *¡Ecue-Yamba-O!* [a Lucumí expression that means something like "God, be praised"]. They gave me provisional freedom. . . . It was then that the term Afro-Cuban came into being. . . . It was, after all, a national awakening. We often witnessed the Ñáñigo *rompimiento* [initiation ceremonies] in Regla.[31]

As has been pointed out by Fernando Alegría, *¡Ecue-Yamba-O!* is "a semidocumentary novel about the primitive magical world of a sector of the black population of Cuba. In it, an important part is played by religious rites, initiation ceremonies, formulas for spells, and by the substratum of Ñáñigo people who live in a stage of collective representation, prelogical and mystical, right in the midst of modern civilization." [32] Thus, as Klaus Müller-Bergh indicates, what predominates in this first novel by Carpentier is "the desire for realism and documentation"; because of this desire and "in spite of the novelty of the theme and certain stylistic innovations, the author was following a road parallel to that of the traditional Spanish-American novel." [33] Indeed, ¡Ecue-Yamba-O! does not represent any substantial innovation in the evolution of the Spanish-American novel; Carpentier follows the formula of man in or facing nature, underlined by the fact that the author identifies the manifestations of religious syncretism of the black with the natural milieu. Rites, magic, and African cosmogonies are part of the landscape, rather than the particular form in which a certain culture faces the phenomena of creation and tries to wrest their secret from them. As Carpentier himself would later say, he had not understood the black's animism or the meaning of the forest in the black's mind.

It is clear that Menegildo Cué, the protagonist, lives in some specific epoch. But it is not a historical epoch, in the strictest sense of the term, nor is it mythical. The author has created a static temporal dimension, the result of the juxtaposition of different periods in the political events of Cuba, unchanging in the story. Thus, the movements of the character are essentially spatial, and this is exaggerated by the fact that the identification produced in the mind of the black among these spaces has more to do with what is than with what is done. I do not mean to say that politics, for example, do not enter into Menegildo's life; but they are always a force alien to him, whose significance he never comes to understand fully. There is no deep realization that he is a man; the passage of time is something he feels, basically, in his biological function, that is, as a natural being.

Nature plays an important role throughout the story. Many are the chapters devoted to describing different types of landscapes, and the description of a tropical cyclone is seventeen pages long, a veritable tour de force in its sustained futuristic style (40–56). Elsewhere, rites and spells function principally to exorcise biological and natural forces, except for the Ñáñigo rompimiento ceremony, which has political connotations and is the most enduring episode of the novel, according to the author. The chapter entitled "El embó" illustrates the association between magic and nature, with Menegildo trying to produce a sexual response in the woman he loves passionately, although what he really wants is to overcome his own timidity with a pretext of witchcraft (86–93). In this passage, we can also observe the stylization with which Carpentier treats the black theme. The conjuration of Beruá, the wizard, becomes a poem in the Afro-Cuban mode:

> The saint in Guinea.
> Sará-yé-yé!
> Usebio on the farm.
> Sará-yé-yé!
> The saint in Guinea.
> Sará-yé-yé!
>
> .   .   .
>
> Menegildo, Menegildo.
> Sará-yé-yé!
> On Luis's farm!
> Sará-yé-yé! Sará-yé-yé! Sára-yé-yé!

We might sum up what we have shown before by pointing out that the guiding forces that inform *¡Ecue-Yamba-O!* are the documentary view of the manifestations of black religious syncretism, a narrative form derived from the criollistas, and an avant-garde style very much contaminated by futurism. From the avant-garde spirit comes the stylization of blackness; and from the documentary zeal comes the creation of a protagonist who develops as a function of the rites. This can be corroborated by Carpentier's later evaluation of this first novel.

> perhaps it is an unsuccessful attempt because of the abuse of metaphors, similes, and images made in the abhorrent bad taste of the futurist, and on account of the concept of nationalism that the men of my generation had at that time. But not everything in it is deplorable. I shall save from the slaughter the chapters devoted to the Ñáñigo ceremony.[34]

In "Problemática de la actual novela hispanoamericana," he makes the following observation about *¡Ecue-Yamba-O!*:

> because I was interested in the practices of *santería* and *Ñáñigu-ismo*, I went to innumerable ritual ceremonies. With this "docu-

mentation," I wrote a novel that was published in Madrid in 1932 [sic], at the height of European nativism. Fine. After twenty years of research into the syncretic realities of Cuba, I realized that all that was deep, true, and universal in the world I had tried to depict in my novel had remained outside the reaches of my observation. For example, the animism of the rural Negro of that period; the relation of the Negro to the forest; certain initiation practices that had been hidden from me by the practitioners with a cleverness that was disconcerting. Since then I have distrusted more and more fundamentally a whole literature which up until recently was being presented to us as the most authentic in America.[35]

For this reason, ¡Ecue-Yambo-O!, a necessary first step in the development of Carpentier's novelistic work, was a learning experience and one that started him off in the direction of an authentically deep and universal expression.

The protagonist is a symbolic synthesis of the rural Cuban black. The story is the cycle of his existence, from the arms of his mother until his death, a cycle that will be repeated in his son—also named Menegildo—whom the hero had left implanted in the womb of Longina before his death. The novel ends where it has begun: with the birth of one of many Menegildos who live in rural Cuba (225). This is why Fernando Alegría was able to write that "Menegildo Cué, in his suffering and death, symbolizes the fate of his race; he goes from exaltation to defeat, from the play of daggers, rhythms, and guitars to the lighted abyss of myths which he consecrates by losing his blood."[36] Thus the character is perceived as an illustration of a segment of the Cuban population, a segment that, in the manner of negrismo, is particularly interesting because of its religious beliefs. And in the last analysis, it is as a function of these beliefs that the character we are analyzing exists.

Carpentier divides his story into three parts, each one longer than the preceding one, which comprise the childhood, adolescence, and early adulthood of the protagonist. At each stage Menegildo is impressed by an initiation that makes him penetrate the mystery more and more deeply. In his childhood it will be his mother's altar; as an adolescent, the fambá chamber of the wizard of the sugar mill; as a man, the extensive ceremonies of the Ñáñigo rompimiento. At each one of these stages of his existence, the spell will function as a therapy for curing sickness and dispelling harmful influences: at the age of three, the bite of a diseased crab; at sixteen, wounds caused by another black. When Menegildo becomes a man, the "devil," a little string of black beads, will be the amulet that subdues the evil forces in his behalf. Finally, the protagonist will sense the social milieu with progressive intensity but without conceptualizing it— the school he cannot attend as a child; his perception as a young fellow of a Republic made up of empty forms; and when he is a man, jail and politicking experiences in the suburbs. As we can see, in the development of his character Carpentier uses a technique of progressive intensification, which suggests a picture of concentric rings that gradually become broader. When the last of these reaches its greatest breadth, it disappears; but the repetition of this phenomenon has already been initiated at the center.

Two forces mark the childhood of Menegildo Cué: Afro-Cuban rites and rhythm. He arrives in the world in circumstances not very different from those of the birth of an animal, and the first significant experience in the formation of his psychology is his initiation into the mysteries of the cult of images. Crawling along slowly, Menegildo, still an infant, has arrived before the family altar, a dazzling discovery:

> suddenly a marvelous discovery changed his tears to joy; from a low table little gilt and brightly-colored statutes were peeking at him. There was one old man on crutches, followed by two dogs with red tongues. A crowned woman, dressed in pure white, with a chubby-cheeked child in her arms. A black figure that brandished an iron ax. Necklaces of green beads. A little bread fastened with a ribbon. A dish full of little round pebbles. [25]

Menegildo Cué, and with him the reader, faces for the first time the pantheon peopled by Afro-Cuban deities. They are still nameless, but they nevertheless exert a deep and powerful attraction. As they take on the appearance of saints of the Catholic calendar, Menegildo's growth as a black man will be identified with the gradual deepening of his understanding of the forces that regulate his existence. These forces can be utilized to personal advantage for various purposes.

Thus, when he suffers some kind of poisoning toward the end of his third year, Beruá, the wizard and the family doctor, will come to his parents' cabin to "throw out the snails," that is, to divine the future course of the sickness, to anoint him with snake grease, and to recite to him the prayer of the "Just Judge" (Carpentier inserts the prayer in its entirety) in order to "protect him for a long time against persecution by men or animals of prey" (26). With these rites, the author begins to unfold his "documentation" of the magical-liturgical practices of the Cuban blacks with an objectivity and precision that remind us of the anthropological studies of this segment of the Cuban population. But from these descriptions one does not get an authentic or distinctive characterization of the individual: Menegildo Cué is not a person; he is a species. Moreover, these beliefs are presented with absolute rigor; they are introduced into the black's psychical makeup like a petrified dogma that impedes the free flow of the fantasy or feelings of the character. There is no mutual inter-action between belief and human being; the only thing practicable for the individual is a mechanical acceptance, although this may be made with a certain fear, stupor, or bedazzlement.

This magical-mythical world is perfected in the protagonist through the skill he shows in expressing it rhythmically. At the age of eight, "Menegildo did not know how to read; he did not even know the art of signing with an x. But on the other hand, he had a doctorate in gestures and motions. The sense of rhythm pulsated in him as did his blood" (33). It is for this reason that the "official culture" will influence his spirit very little; the boy is perceived as the product of an ancestral line that shapes him fundamentally and is expressed in his aptitude for interpreting the secret "beats" of the tom-tom:

> By racial inheritance he knew the yambú, the long, rustic sounds, and he divined the science that made the "saint step down." In a nervous rumba he produced all the movements of a dancing couple with his shadow. Light-headed, with a serious look and his eyes on an axletree, he let his shoulders gravitate toward an invisible axis embedded in his navel. He gave sudden leaps. His hands opened, palms down. His feet glided along the rammed earth of the doorway, and the outlines of his body were changed at every step. Anatomy subjected to the dance of ancestral instinct! [38]

By the time he is sixteen, Menegildo is already a strapping and well-formed youth; "his muscles responded to the labor imposed on them like chess pieces of excellent human quality" (59). But it is his spiritual life that interests the novelist most deeply; after having described him as a pure black descended from *carabalis,* Carpentier introduces us to the adolescent, already instructed in the mysteries of "the things" by his mother and immersed in black mythology. Menegildo believes there are hidden designs that are beyond man's comprehension and, when he thinks of the world of secrets that has been revealed to him, he is surprised at his smallness and weakness before the "vast harmony of hidden forces. . . . In that world what one could see amounted to very little. Earthly creatures lived beguiled under the merciful gaze of superior entities. Oh, Yemayá, Shangó, y Obatalá, spirits of infinite perfection! . . . But among men there were secret bonds, powers that could be mobilized for an understanding of their secret origins" (60).

Menegildo has a mystical vision of existence. For him, fundamental wisdom consists in overcoming the apparent phenomena that surround us, which are of little import in any case, and in living in acceptance of mystery, with the assurance that those "superior entities" regard us with compassion, taking account of our human imperfections. Besides, among men there are "secret bonds" that can be controlled through an esoteric knowledge of their sources. Thus, theology and magic are solidly fused in this "really simple soul," which is, moreover, capable only of "expressing happiness, surprise, indifference, pain, or lubricity" (59). Accordingly, the deep magical-mystical being of Menegildo seeks the support of the powers in order to possess Longina. Now he is going to be initiated into the mystery of an authentic *fambá* chamber, during the "despoliation" ceremonies and the preparation of the *embó:* "Palpitating with emotion, mute, sweating, Menegildo went into the sanctuary followed by the wise Beruá. . . . A shudder of terror went up and down Menegildo's spine. . . . For the first time he found himself standing before the 'big' things, of which the altar of Salomé, his mother, seemed but a very weak reflection" (89).

As can be appreciated, the character has arrived at a new, deeper dimension of the mystery as he becomes an object of esoteric liturgy. This permits Carpentier, in accord with his desire to document and illustrate, an opportunity to pass on to a detailed description of a rural *fambá* chamber and the despoliation ceremonies. But the protagonist passes into a secondary role when he becomes a passive recipient of the rite; what is presented is the external description of the magic act, not the impression the ceremony makes on the boy. In other words, there is much in the characterization of Menegildo that is expedient, put there so that the novelist can display all the "paraphernalia" of the Cuban black cult of images.

A result of this ceremony is Menegildo's initiation into the sexual act. With Longina, Menegildo "enamored like a horse" (104), does not surpass the level of pure instinct; his relations with her are like the elemental ones between a male and a female animal. And as a male, he must defend his mate from the Haitian black "Napolión." The consequences of Menegildo's fight with Napolión are an accident that almost costs the protagonist his life and then jail. But the author's ultimate objective is to place Menegildo in a new, even deeper dimension of the African magical-mythical world. Accordingly, the spells that Beruá recites over his half-dying body are much more complicated, given the gravity of the situation, than those he had pronounced when Menegildo had suffered from *ciguatera* (a sickness) at three years. First, the wizard throws into the air the "Ifá necklace," studying the position into which the sixteen half mango seeds fall, in order to find out whether the sick man "will go back onto the road which will take him to the world of phantoms and presages" (111). Then he proceeds to the application of a therapy based on a mixture of cobwebs and the omnipresent panacea, snake grease (112).

In the jail in the capital, where he has been put after stabbing Napolión, Menegildo comes into contact with some "true Ñáñigos" who even initiate him into some knowledge of the "tongue" (140). His cousin Antonio, a member of one of these associations, also instructs him, when he visits him in jail, in the history of these secret brotherhoods that have their roots in the mythical African past, although now (in the early twentieth century) they are electoral instruments in the hands of the political bosses: "in the city that surrounded the prison there were two gangs, hereditary enemies, the Efó-Abacana and the Enellegüellé. Equally protected by the mayor, who had voters in their ranks, they had confirmed their prestige with acts of war" (158). Antonio, a member of the second gang, obtains freedom for Menegildo through his influence with "Councillor Uñita," a Ñáñigo of the Enellegüellé group (1962).

The protagonist becomes affiliated with this brotherhood in a ceremony that lasts eighteen hours and takes up three chapters of the story. But, as in the fambá chamber, Menegildo's only reaction during this ordeal is of fear in the face of mystery (175), an emotion that is, moreover, very superficially analyzed. Again the hero disappears under the weight of the black liturgy, because what interests Carpentier is the narration of the initiation rite in all its details—the flourishes, the different drumbeats, the instruments of the cult, the magic words, the sacred potions, the consecrated garments, the dances, the emblems, the Ñáñigo features, as well as the animal sacrifices and the contests in the speaking of the "tongue." The stages in the ceremony, in its most minute components, are described with the accuracy of an ethnologist. We get the impression that Menegildo has faded out of the story, not buried under the mass of those being initiated but lost in the detailed description of the ceremony. Any human dimension there may be is diluted; what stands out is the objective exposition of the secret rite:

> The new ones got up. Each one was led by his sponsor up to the entrance of the cabin, where they were awaited by the Munifambá of the Potentate [the priest of the gods]. . . . The Munifambá entrusted the neophytes to the Iyamba. The latter walked solemnly to the back of the room and opened a secret door that led to the Fambá Chamber. The neophytes were taken into the sanctuary one by one and were made to kneel before an altar that they still would not see for a long time: a table covered with red paper, surrounded with paper flowers and offerings in chocolate cups and tin cans. [177–78]

As can be clearly seen, the rite makes the characters, especially the neophytes, sacerdotal to the point of making them lose their human features. The initiates thus come to be one more element in the story. Because the author underplays any tone of individuality in the liturgical celebration, he does not succeed in expressing a truly sacred attitude.

Accordingly, Menegildo Cué has come into contact with all the manifestations of the cult of images and of Ñáñigism. His novelistic cycle is completed when all his possibilities for illustrating the beliefs and religious practices of the Cuban blacks have been exhausted. Because he is a character conceived as a function of the rite, all that remains is for him to confirm in his own flesh the fidelity to which he has sworn himself. And so he comes to his death. "The prisoner of ancestral forces which, without the fervor or prestige of the ancient myth, move around in the suburban culvert under the tainted light of old street lamps, to the rhythm of damp drums and in a mist of cheap liquor, Menegildo falls with his jugular vein cut." [37]

If *¡Ecue-Yamba-O!* is fundamentally a text illustrative of the magical-mythical compass of the Cuban black, in which the protagonist is conceived as a progressive expression of such beliefs, in *El reino de este mundo* (1949), on the contrary, the religious vision is directed toward illuminating the character, who in his turn is conceived as a vehicle for clarifying human destiny. It is obvious that the point of view and the purpose of the novelist have changed. Menegildo Cué was interesting as a believer in a ritual and a theology; Ti Noel, confined to his tellurian and epicopolitical context, interests us because of his possibilities for defining the task and the being of man. In addition, the story that concerns us here takes for granted a broadening of Carpentier's theme choices, which before were limited to types and subjects from the reality of his own country; also, with regard to technique, the story shows a new method of novel writing, involving the abandonment of the old criollista formula. On this subject, Klaus Müller-Bergh has written that the "tendency toward magic realism which appears in *Viaje a la semilla* attains its full realization in *El reino de este mundo*." [38]

In this "story of magic and voodoo which has Haiti as its scene, and which has an architecture and style related to surrealistic works," [39] Carpentier develops the life experience of a black slave, Ti Noel, under three kinds of tyranny. The novel includes events from the last years of the French domination of the island until the installation of a "Mulatto Republic," including the fabulous reign of Henri Christophe. It is a succession of extraordinary and marvelous incidents, which however come from a strictly historical reality that the author followed in all its details. As the author comments in his prologue, "the very story you are going to read has been based on an extremely rigorous documentation, which not only respects the historical truth of the incidents, the names of the characters—even the secondary ones—the places and even the streets but which also hides beneath its apparent timelessness a precise collation of dates and chronologies.[40]

This blending of the marvelous and the historical, in its apparent timelessness, forms a new kind of historical novel, which Salvador Bueno chooses to call a "legendary chronicle."[41] Fernando Alegría has observed that "history in the hands of Carpentier acquires an atmosphere of madness, a frenzy of nightmarish movement, a wealth of associations that affect both the senses and the intellect. The world of violence . . . emerges as schematic, direct, and fascinating. It lives in a language of such vibrant symbols . . . that the story issues spontaneously from history and stands there looking at us with all the faces of its multiple reality."[42]

All the techniques the author uses in this novel are directed toward clarifying the nature of the kingdom of this world and of the human condition. In the last analysis, the novel proposes to answer two fundamental questions: What is man, and what is the nature of his mission? Thus, it breaks spacial and temporal boundaries and achieves a universal dimension. In accordance with this view, the life experience of Ti Noel is conceived in such a way as to bring about a progressive awareness in the character of the intrinsic human attributes that the author wishes to reveal. The hero, placed in and suffering in a very specific historic period, is defined by the context that bounds him; but when one arrives at the relationship that unifies these elements, he is reaching man's ultimate root, atemporal and metaphysical. Thus, the protagonist is interesting, not on account of the color of his skin or on account of the exotic and picturesque features of his culture, but because of his fundamental condition as a human being, which allows his individual existence to acquire a supraracial and universal scope.

It is in this way that marvelous reality, as it is defined by Carpentier in his prologue (12–13), because it follows an authentic expressive need, is intimately tied to the core of the plot and consequently comes to form a part of the characterization of the protagonist. "Carpentier's magic realism," Alegría has written, "does not contain a romantic kind of idealization; his realism rests on a recording of historical facts, which are transformed into legends in the imagination of the people, and which then have the same function as myths derived from a collective subconscious." [43] For example, the metamorphoses of Mackandal and his fantastic salvation become sure facts in the mind of the slaves, so that Ti Noel, in a moment of dejection, tries metamorphosis as a means of escaping from his "vesture" as a man. But it is through these "transformations" that the protagonist comes to the profound realization that it is impossible to avoid one's own destiny, even if human appearances are abandoned. In other words, the technique of magic realism serves to confront the hero with his essence and to force him to arrive at a philosophical understanding of the human being.

Another aspect of marvelous reality can be seen in the first chapter of this story. Ti Noel, as he confused in his mind the waxen heads exhibited in a barbershop with the skinned calves' heads shown for sale in a contiguous commercial establishment, "amused himself thinking that the heads of white men were being served beside the discolored heads of veal at the same table" (20). The influence of surrealism can clearly be seen here; but from this unusual association of very diverse elements of reality comes a possibility of action on the part of the black man, an action which has its root in a subconscious desire. Also, the substance of the bloody events that will happen later is contained in this motif. We have here, then, an "auspicious illumination of the unexpected richness of reality" (12), with which the author is showing us the character in his context. Ti Noel is defined by means of an "outside-inside operation." This is a new procedure in the characterization of the black protagonist. Although at the beginning of the novel Carpentier alludes to the youth of the slave (21) and later, upon his return from Santiago de Cuba, describes him as "old but still firm on his scaly feet, covered with bunions" (94), in this story the author has given up the tedious enumerations of the so-called realism of the nineteenth century. He has rid himself of any annoying inventory of physical details and psychological minutiae in order to create the character by means of shattering illustrations from a reality whose deepest truths have been penetrated. These truths have been penetrated precisely by means of the relationships the author establishes, a fact that causes a constant movement from the accidental to the essential and in the last analysis makes possible the transcendental scope of *El reino de este mundo*.

Possessed of a cultural heritage in which knowing consists of the apprehension of the ultimate and elemental reality of the world around us, Ti Noel has the capacity to discern the value of things. This wisdom, alogical and almost instinctive, comes to him from the ancestral truths he has learned from Mackandal (23), which lead him to establish a hierarchy in his own judgment of the world. Thus, for example, the black man senses the inconsistency of the white rulers "covered with alien skins, who bowled and who knew how to create gods only in their court theaters, showing off their effeminate legs to the rhythm of a quadrille" (22). On the contrary, in the "great Beyond," "there were princes as hard as an anvil, and princes who were leopards, and princes who knew the language of the trees, and princes who ruled the four corners of the earth, masters of the clouds, the seeds, of copper and fire" (23). Ti Noel's evaluation also defines the character in his context, at the same time explaining the source of the incidents that are about to happen.

Clearly, what Ti Noel is constantly seeking is authenticity. But we should be badly mistaken if we associated this authenticity with the realm of tangible objects. To the slave there are mysterious forces outside the domain of our senses but just as real as the phenomena we can perceive. These forces issue from the "High Powers of the Other Shore"; they constantly evade the whites, who are incapable of understanding these things (50). Likewise, the lycanthropical forces, the metamorphoses, the marvelous acts, and, in general, the various manifestations of voodoo that appear throughout the story evade them. But these forces are closely tied to the epicopolitical context of *El reino de este mundo*, for, as M. Lenormand Mezy, Ti Noel's master, thinks, "The slaves had a secret religion that encouraged them and gave them solidarity in their rebellions" (71). Thus, the magical-mystical conception the blacks have of the world has a different function in this novel than it had in *¡Ecue-Yamba-O!* The "secret religion" acquires a historical and universal sense when it is a function of one of man's highest aspirations. Voodoo is seen, therefore, in terms that go beyond the illustration of the native and picturesque that had been the purpose of describing the cult of images and Ñáñigism in the Afro-Cuban story. Carpentier has presented it to us from a supraracial and ecumenical perspective, thus classifying those who practice it as human beings. The black has ceased to be an ethnic curiosity or a piquant decorative element of a decadent cultural posture. This statement is corroborated by the swearing-in ceremony, the "highest pact," concluded between the initiates from America and the great Loas from Africa. As Bouckman says in his speech; "The God of the white men orders crime. Our gods ask vengeance of us. They will guide our hands and give us assistance. May they break the image of the god of the whites, who thirsts after our tears; may we hear in ourselves the call to liberty!" (61).

The protagonist will experience more and more deeply this human and universal dimension. When he returns from Santiago de Cuba he will become aware of the tremendous irony in the rule of Henri Christophe, a slavery just as abominable as he had known on his old master's hacienda: "Even worse, since there was infinite misery in seeing himself cudgeled by a Negro as black as he, as thick-lipped, crisp-haired and flat-nosed as he; a man as indifferent, as low-born, and possibly as much branded as he" (107). His sad experience at Sans-Souci was the beginning of his realization that he had a mission to perform—"something great, something worthy of the rights acquired by a person who has had so many years' residence in this world" (147). However, when he is obliged to suffer the ultimate tyranny, the Mulatto Republic, "desperate in the face of the untiring reappearance of chains" (51), he decides to get rid of his human vesture and metamorphose himself into a bird, a stallion, a wasp, an ant, and a goose, as Mackandal had done before.The disagreeable experiences he has in each one of these states make him comprehend, as we have seen, the impossibility of escaping his own human destiny. He thus understands that Mackandal "had disguised himself as an animal for many years in order to serve men" (165). In this way he arrives at his final wisdom:

> man's greatness lies precisely in wanting to better himself. In imposing tasks upon himself. In the Kingdom of the Heavens there is no greatness to acquire, since there all is an established hierarchy, an unknown quantity clear of obstructions, an endless existence, with no possibility for sacrifice, repose, or delight. For this reason, bowed down with hardships and tasks, beautiful in the midst of his misery, capable of loving in the middle of plagues, man finds his greatness, his highest stature, only in the Kingdom of this World [156].

After having made his "declaration of war against the new masters," Ti Noel disappears, swept away by the symbolic chaos of a tropical cyclone (157). One individual destiny has served as a guide to the understanding of man's task, and thus the novel acquires its ultimate meaning. With Ti Noel, Carpentier overcomes spacial-temporal limitation and reaches the ultimate reality, the universal essence that resides in each human being. Thus it is that in *¡Ecue-Yamba-O!*, when he balances and liquidates his debt to criollismo, the protagonist is placed in space, in nature, whereas in the novel of Haiti, without losing his relation to the earthly context, the principal character is an integral part of time, of history. Moreover, if we compare the two stories, we can observe a different treatment of the ritual, mystical, and magical elements of black culture.

The characterization of the black protagonist during the first fifty years of the Republic has shown a constant tendency to overcome technical artlessness. At the same time, the black character has grown in excellence. Through the use of the expressive developments of avant-gardism and surrealism, the black as a fictional character has transcended the purely local and typicalist and has entered the realm of the universal. In this way, *El negrero*, with its fundamental objectivism, and *¡Ecue-Yamba-O!*, with its effort to penetrate the mythical root of the Cuban black, transcend the superficial picturesqueness of *Mersé*. At the same time, in *Caniquí* and *El reino de este mundo*, because the protagonist has an essentially human function, the character goes beyond the limits of geography and race. In these last two novels, the black is interesting not as a black but as a person, thereby acquiring truly universal value. And that is what is really important.

Summary

The analysis of the characterization of the black protagonist in the Cuban novel allows us to point out several facts we think may be significant.

First of all, we note a marked difference in the evolution that takes place in the characterization of heroes and heroines.

In the novels studied, the black or mulatto fits one of two basic types that show no significant alteration: on the one hand, the idealized image of the slave woman, a person of extreme purity, the object of economic and sexual exploitation, subject to the absolute and arbitrary will of her white masters; on the other, the stereotype of the free mulatto, an ingenuous person with primitive passions whose ultimate objective, never realized, is to be integrated into and respected by white society. Both types share one basic feature; they point up the perversity of a system that robs them of their essential humanity. The pathos of these fictional characters lies in the impossibility of their escaping their function as machines for production, concubines, or criminals. They are passive victims, whose behavior always has the same level of meaning: they are the depositories of the injustice and evil of a caste system that has reduced them to objects of pleasure, leading lives of toil, pain, and sadness. Their existence is a series of misfortunes leading to violent death, insanity, or crime. As a result, the depiction of these characters serves as a moral judgment of the society that oppresses them.

On the contrary, other dimensions are added to the characterization process undergone by the black male protagonist. He also is seen as a victim of the society that oppresses him, but unlike the female protagonist, he takes on a rebellious character (both internally and externally) and a politicization that grows stronger until he becomes a symbol of Cuban nationality and of the human condition in general. In sum, these male figures are not just passive victims; they are people who can conceptualize, one way or another, their vision of the universe and propose that vision to us as a possible solution to specific historical conflicts. The progressive enrichment we see in the characterization of the black hero, in contrast to the static stereotype of the heroine, reflects the double slavery of the latter—slavery of race and of sex. This truth can be observed in *Sab* by Gertrudis Gómez de Avellaneda. The abolitionism of the author corresponds to her feminism; her white heroine is subjected to a tyranny that converts her also into a passive victim.

In all the writers studied, there is an obvious political and social awareness, variable in its intensity and acuteness but always a decisive factor and a motive that leads them to bring the black character into their stories. Thus, it comes about that the novel about blacks in Cuba is *engagé* literature, if we understand this term in the broad sense. We have not perceived any substantial opposition between *engagement* and aesthetic quality; quite the contrary, we have noted that the efficacy of the expression is in direct relationship to the identification established between the author and the character. This level of identification, we believe, has determined the methods of characterization employed by the novelists. These methods, if it is indeed true that they can be associated with the narrative techniques of Western fiction, go outside the limits of conventional historicoliterary classifications.

The novelists studied have tried to capture the black character by utilizing three basic forms. Suárez Romero, Avellaneda, and Morúa Delgado have remained faithful to an aesthetic and a sensibility or ideology that belong to a certain age; hence, their novels and characters have a tendency toward "schoolish" erudition. For their part, Villaverde, Calcagno, Meza, and Soloni have, in very diverse aesthetic forms and attainments, concerned themselves with expressing typical and differentiating features, with the result that they have produced a markedly costumbrista picture of the black, a reflection of the social consensus. Finally, Zambrana, Ramos, and Carpentier, starting with personal and differentiating features, have tried to discover the universal in their characters. In these last novelists, we observe an antidogmatic and broad aesthetic attitude, tending toward the syncretic and therefore typically Spanish American. These writers, especially Ramos and Carpentier, have succeeded in revealing a character with supraracial significance.

Such is the lesson we have learned in the course of our work. In studying the black in literature, it is not important to point out the relative skill of the author in capturing the black's differentiating ethnic and cultural features; that would be an extremely narrow criterion for interpretation. What matters essentially is to show how well the author has succeeded in expressing the human and universal transcendency of a way of being, of a particular world view that enriches us all. For only to the extent that the creative author has overcome an epidermal and limited vision of the blacks, delving into their authentic human inwardness, has he succeeded in understanding them as human beings and therefore in presenting them to us as true fictional creations.

Notes

Chapter One

1. Ramiro Guerra, *Manual de historia de Cuba* (Havana, 1962), p. 43.
2. José A. Saco, *Historia de la esclavitud* (Paris, 1975), 4: 75.
3. Guerra, *Manual*, p. 43.
4. Ibid., p. 48.
5. Saco, *Historia*, 4: 75.
6. Emeterio S. Santovenia and Raúl M. Shelton, *Cuba y su historia* (Miami, 1965), 1: 139.
7. Ibid., p. 140.
8. Ibid., p. 147.
9. Guerra, *Manual*, p. 89.
10. Ibid., p. 89.
11. Ibid., p. 93.
12. Santovenia and Shelton, *Cuba*, 1: 160, 206.
13. Guerra, *Manual*, p. 122.
14. Ibid., p. 185.
15. "Documentos de que hasta ahora se compone el expediente que principiaron las Cortes Extraordinarias sobre el tráfico y la esclavitud de los negros," quoted by Angel Rosenblat in *La población indígena (1492–1950)* (Buenos Aires, 1954), p. 118.
16. José A. Saco, *Papeles sobre Cuba* (Havana, 1960), 1: 405–26.
17. Francisco Coello, *Atlas de España y sus posesiones de ultramar,* s. v. "Cuba" (Madrid, 1851).
18. Alberto Arredondo, *El negro en Cuba* (Havana, 1939), pp. 29–30.
19. Guerra, *Manual*, p. 247.
20. Santovenia and Shelton, *Cuba*, 1: 241–42.
21. Guerra, *Manual*, p. 235.
22. Rosenblat, *La población*, p. 186.
23. Arredondo, *El negro*, pp. 29–30.

24. Guerra, *Manual,* p. 247.
25. Ibid., p. 313.
26. Saco, *Papeles sobre Cuba,* 1: 174.
27. Arredondo, *El negro,* pp. 29–30.
28. Guerra, *Manual,* p. 411.
29. Loló de la Torriente, *La Habana de Cecilia Valdés* (Havana, 1946), p. 77.
30. Fernando Ortiz, *Los negros esclavos* (Havana, 1916), p. 23.
31. Alejandro de Humboldt, *Ensayo político sobre la isla de Cuba* (Havana, 1930), 2: 66.
32. Torriente, *La Habana,* p. 77.
33. Guerra, *Manual,* p. 413.
34. Ibid., p. 428.
35. Vidal Morales y Morales, *Iniciadores y primeros mártires de la revolución cubana* (Havana, 1931), 1: 288.
36. Guerra, *Manual,* p. 446.
37. See Cirilo Villaverde, *Cecilia Valdés* (New York, 1964), p. 233.
38. Coello, *Atlas,* s. v. *"Cuba";* Arredondo, *El negro,* pp. 29–30.
39. Arrendondo, *El negro,* p. 29.
40. Guerra, *Manual,* p. 449.
41. Ibid., p. 646.
42. Santovenia and Shelton, *Cuba* 2: 22–24.
43. Emilio Roig de Leuchsenring, *La Habana, apuntes históricos* (Havana, 1963), p. 41.
44. Rosenblat, *La población,* p. 146.
45. Fernando Ortiz, *Los negros brujos* (Madrid, n.d.), p. 35.

Chapter Two

1. José A. Fernández de Castro, *El tema negro en las letras de Cuba* (Havana, 1943); Raymond S. Sayers, *The Negro in Brazilian Literature* (New York, 1956); Gregory Rabassa, *The Negro in Brazilian Fiction since 1888* (New York, 1954).
2. For instance, he changes the names of Domingo del Monte and Antonio Zambrana and maintains that Gabriel de la Concepción Valdés, "Plácido," was born a slave (G. R. Coulthard, *Raza y color en la literatura antillana* [Seville, 1958], pp. 8, 14, 27).
3. See Aurelio Mitjans, *Estudio sobre el movimiento científico y literario de Cuba* (Havana, 1963), p. 59.
4. Silvestre de Balboa, *Espejo de paciencia,* ed. Cintio Vitier (Universidad Central de las Villas, Cuba, 1960), pp. 82–84.
5. Ramón Guirao, *Orbita de la poesía afrocubana* (Havana, 1938), p. xix.
6. Fernando Ortiz, *La antigua fiesta afrocubana del "Día de Reyes"* (Havana, 1960), p. 41.
7. Guirao, *Orbita,* pp. 7–9.
8. Antonio López Prieto, *Parnaso cubano* (Havana, 1881), pp. liv–lv; also

quoted by Max Henríquez Ureña, *Panorama histórico de la literatura cubana* (New York, 1963), 1:77n.58.

9. Carlos M. Trelles, *Bibliografía cubana de los siglos XVII y XVIII* (Havana, 1927), p. 219.

10. Guirao, *Orbita*, p. xxv.

11. Juan F. Manzano, *Autobiografía versos y cartas* (Havana, 1937), p. 92.

12. Fernández de Castro, *El tema negro*, p. 32.

13. Also quoted by Emilio Ballagas, *Mapa de la poesía negra americana* (Buenos Aires, 1946), p. 98. Many of the poems quoted in this chapter are taken from the anthologies of Ballagas and Guirao and from Cintio Vitier, *Cincuenta años de poesía cubana* (Havana, 1952). When the poems are taken from a different source, this fact will be indicated.

14. José M. Chacón y Calvo, *Las cien mejores poesías cubanas* (Madrid, 1922), p. 59.

15. López Prieto, *Parnaso*, p. 81.

16. José J. Milanés, *Obras completas* (Havana, 1920), 1: 44.

17. Ballagas, *Mapa*, p. 99.

18. Chacón y Calvo, *Las cien poesías*, p. 254.

19. José Martí, *Obras completas* (Havana, 1953), 1: 499, 487.

20. Coulthard, *Raza*, p. 31.

21. Ballagas, *Mapa*, p. 86.

22. Roberto Fernández Retamar, *La poesia contemporánea en Cuba (1927–1953)* (Havana, 1954), p. 47.

23. Ballagas, *Mapa*, p. 86.

24. José Juan Arrom, *Historia de la literatura dramática cubana* (New Haven, 1944), p. 35.

25. Ibid., p. 61.

26. See José A. Escarpenter, Presentación, *Panorama histórico del teatro cubano* (Havana, 1965), pp. 60–64.

27. Ureña, *Panorama* (Havana, 1965), p. 65.

28. Arrom, *Historia*, p. 64.

29. Fernández de Castro, *El tema negro*, p. 68.

30. Ibid., p. 73.

31. Also quoted by Fernández de Castro, ibid., p. 75.

32. See Fernández Retamar, *La poesía*, p. 45.

33. Vitier, *Cincuenta años*, p. 219.

34. Guirao, *Orbita*, p. 45.

35. José Juan Arrom, "La poesía afrocubana," in *Estudios de literatura hispanoamericana* (Havana, 1950).

36. Guirao, *Orbita*, p. xix; Arrom, *Estudios*, p. 122.

37. Guirao, *Orbita*, p. xix.

38. Vitier, *Cincuenta años*, p. 188.

39. Fernández Retamar, *La poesía*, p. 49.

40. Vitier, *Cincuenta años*, p. 229.

41. Fernández Retamar, *La poesía*, p. 57.

42. Arrom, *Historia*, p. 89.

43. Natividad González Freire, *Teatro cubano, 1927–1961* (Havana, 1961), p. 157.
44. Arrom, *Historia*, p. 157.
45. Ibid., p. 89.
46. González Freire, *Teatro*, p. 18.
47. Paco Alfonso, *Yari-Yari, mamá Olúa* (Havana, 1941).
48. Arrom, *Historia*, p. 86.
49. Fernández de Castro, *El tema negro*, p. 88.
50. Alejo Carpentier, "Variaciones sobre un tema cubano," *Americas* 2 (March 1950): 21. Also quoted by Klaus Müller-Bergh, "Alejo Carpentier; autor y obra en su época," *Revista iberoamericana* 33 (January-June 1967): 14.

Chapter Three

1. José Juan Arrom, *Esquema generacional de las letras hispanoamericanas* (Bogotá, 1963), p. 19.
2. Raimundo Lazo, *La teoría de las generaciones y su aplicación al estudio histórico de la literatura cubana* (Havana, 1954), p. 32.
3. Quoted by Loló de la Torriente, *La Habana de Cecilia Valdés* (Havana, 1946), p. 77.
4. See *Cuba contemporánea* 39 (December 1925): 287–88.
5. *Centón epistolario de Domingo del Monte* (Havana, 1957), 7: 113.
6. Ibid.
7. Ibid.
8. Ibid.
9. Ibid., p. 114.
10. Ibid.
11. *Cuba contemporánea* 39 (December 1925): 255–88.
12. *Centón*, 7: 115.
13. Ibid., pp. 113–14.
14. Félix M. Tanco y Bosmoniel, *Petrona y Rosalía, Cuba contemporánea* 39 (December 1925): 255. Subsequent references to this work will be made parenthetically in the text.
15. Max Henriquez Ureña, *Panorama histórico de la literatura cubana* (New York, 1963), 1: 235; Juan J. Remos y Rubio, *Historia de la literatura cubana* (Havana, 1945), 2: 205.
16. *Centón*, 7: 114.
17. José L. Franco, "Estudio preliminar," in Juan F. Manzano, *Autobiografía, versos y cartas* (Havana, 1937).
18. Manzano, *Autobiografía*, p. 85.
19. Ibid., p. 28.
20. Henríquez Ureña, *Panorama*, 1: 184–85.
21. Quoted by Franco, "Estudio preliminar," p. 29.
22. Manzano, *Autobiografía*, pp. 83–84.
23. Ibid., p. 85.

24. Ibid.
25. Ibid., pp. 40–41.
26. Ibid., pp. 38–39
27. Ibid., pp. 43–45.
28. Ibid., p. 39.
29. Ibid., pp. 56–57.

Chapter Four

1. Max Henríquez Ureña, *Panorama histórico de la literatura cubana* (New York, 1963), 1: 226.
2. *Evolución de la cultura cubana* (Havana, 1928), 13: 4.
3. Those interested in literary history may consult Henriquez Ureña, *Panorama*, 1: 221–22, n. 177. According to this scholar, if we take into consideration the date of publication, then the first abolitionist novel in the New World would be *Sab* (1841) by G. Gomez de Avellaneda. However, if we take into account the date of composition, then the first abolitionist novel would be Tanco's *Petrona y Rosalía.*
4. José Juan Arrom, *Esquema generacional de las letras* (Bogotá, 1963), p. 19.
5. Ramiro Guerra, *Manual de historia de Cuba* (Havana, 1962), p. 343.
6. See Raimundo Lazo, *La teoría de las generaciones* . . . (Havana, 1954), pp. 35–36.
7. G R. Coulthard, *Raza y color en la literatura antillana* (Seville, 1958), p. 29.
8. Anselmo Suárez y Romero, *Francisco* (Havana, 1947).
9. Ibid., Advertencia, p. 39.
10. Ibid., p. 181, note by Anselmo Suárez y Romero.
11. Ibid., Advertencia, pp. 41, 40.
12. Mario Cabrera Saqui, "Vida, pasión, y gloria de Anselmo Suárez y Romero," in ibid., p. 21.
13. *Centón epistolario de Domingo del Monte* (Havana, 1930), 4: 38–39; also quoted by Cabrera Saqui, "Vida," p. 23.
14. Suárez y Romero, *Francisco,* p. 50. Subsequent references to this work will be made parenthetically in the text.
15. *Centón,* 4: 44–45; also quoted by Cabrera Saqui, "Vida," p. 34.
16. Cabrera Saqui, "Vida," p. 24.
17. Aurelio Mitjans, *Estudio sobre el movimiento científico y literario de Cuba* (Havana, 1963), p. 188.
18. Cirilo Villaverde, *Cecilia Valdés* (New York, 1964), p. 50. Subsequent references to the work will be made parenthetically in the text.
19. Manuel de la Cruz, "Cirilo Villaverde," in *Cromitos cubanos* (Madrid, 1926), p. 175.
20. Manuel de la Cruz, "Cecilia Valdés," in *Obras completas* (Madrid, 1926), 3: 193.
21. Enrique José Varona, "El autor de *Cecilia Valdés,*" *El Figaro* 10 (Novem-

ber 1894): 514; reprinted in *Homenaje a Cirilo Villaverde* (Havana, 1964), p. 102.

22. Diego Vicente Tejera, "Una novela cubana," in *Un poco de prosa* (Havana, 1895), p. 26.
23. Martin Morúa Delgado, *Impresiones literarias: Las novelas del señor Villaverde* (Havana, 1892); reprinted in *Homenaje a Cirilo Villaverde*, p. 128.
24. Marguerite C. Suárez-Murias, *La novela romántica en Hispanoamérica* (New York, 1963), p. 37.
25. Morúa Delgado, *Impresiones*, p. 122.
26. Coulthard, *Raza*, p. 19.
27. Morúa Delgado, *Impresiones*, p. 127.
28. Cruz, "Cecilia Valdés," 3: 195.
29. Enrique Anderson-Imbert, *Historia de la literatura hispanoamericana* (Mexico, 1962), 1: 248.
30. "Apuntes biográficos"; also quoted by Emilio Cotarelo y Mori, *La Avellaneda y sus obras* (Madrid, 1930), p. 23.
31. Published by Cotarelo, *La Avellaneda*, pp. 248–430.
32. Gertrudis Gómez de Avellaneda, *Memorias* (1838) published by Domingo Figarola-Caneda, *Gertrudis Gómez de Avellaneda* (Madrid, 1929), pp. 249–92.
33. Gertrudis Gómez de Avellaneda, *Sab*, 2 vols. (Madrid, 1841). Subsequent references to this work will be made parenthetically in the text.
34. Gertrudis Gómez de Avellaneda, *Autobiografía y cartas*, ed. Lorenzo Cruz de Fuentes (Huelva, 1907), p. 56.
35. Gómez de Avellaneda, *Autobiografía*, p. 84.
36. Published by Figarola-Caneda, *Gómez de Avellaneda*, p. 151.
37. See Gómez de Avellaneda, *Autobiografía*, pp. 35, 36, 53, and 64; also Figarola-Caneda, *Gómez de Avellaneda*, p. 258.
38. Helena Percas Ponseti, "Sobre la Avellaneda y su novela *Sab*," *Revista iberoamericana* 38 (1962): 347–57.
39. Also quoted by Cotarelo, *La Avellaneda*, p. 75, and Percas Ponseti, "Sobre la Avellaneda," p. 349.
40. Cotarelo, *La Avellaneda*, p. 75; Percas Ponseti, "Sobre la Avellaneda," p. 349.
41. Percas Ponseti, "Sobre la Avellaneda," pp. 357, 354.
42. Mitjans, *Estudio*, p. 197.
43. José A. Portuondo, *Bosquejo histórico de las letras cubanas* (Havana, 1960), p. 30; Lorenzo García Vega, *Antologia de las novela cubana* (Havana, 1960), p. 49.
44. Raymond S. Sayers, *The Negro in Brazilian Literature* (New York, 1956), p. 26.
45. Ibid., p. 38.
46. Biographical information taken from the jacket of Francisco Calcagno's historical book, *Aponte* (Barcelona, 1901).
47. Francisco Calcagno, *Romualdo: Uno de tantos* (Havana, 1891), p. 85. Subsequent references to the work will be made parenthetically in the text.

Chapter Five

1. Raimundo Lazo, *La teoría de las generaciones* . . . (Havana, 1954), p. 37.
2. José Juan Arrom, *Esquema generacional de las letras* (Bogotá, 1963), p. 19.
3. Lazo, *La teoría*, p. 39.
4. Ibid., p. 37.
5. Antonio Zambrana Vásquez, *El negro Francisco* (Havana, 1948), p. 5. Subsequent references to this work will be made parenthetically· in the text.
6. Also quoted by G. R. Coulthard, *Raza y color en la literatura antillana* (Seville, 1958), p. 29.
7. Ibid., p. 30.
8. See Manuel de la Cruz, "Ramón Meza," in *Cromitos cubanos* (Madrid, 1926), p. 264; Juan J. Remos y Rubio, *Historia de la literatura cubana* (Havana, 1945), 2: 569; Max Henríques Ureña, *Panorama historico de la literatura cubana* (New York, 1963), 2: 168.
9. Cruz, "Ramón Meza," p. 261.
10. Ramón Meza, *Carmela* (Havana, 1886), p. 123. Subsequent references to this work will be made parenthetically in the text.
11. Cruz, "Ramón Meza," p. 264.
12. Henríquez Ureña, *Panorama*, 2: 106.
13. Only his second novel reached publication: *La familia de Unzúazo* (1896).
14. Henríquez Ureña, *Panorama*, 2: 105.
15. Martín Morúa Delgado, *Sofía* (Havana, 1891), p. 239. Subsequent references to this work will be made parenthetically in the text.
16. Nineteenth-century Cuban society produced various examples of this phenomenon. See Francisco Calcagno, *Aponte* (Barcelona, 1901), pp. 207–12.

Chapter Six

1. Félix Lizaso, *Ensayistas contemporáneos* (Havana, 1938), p. 10; Raimundo Lazo, *La teoría de las generaciones* . . . (Havana, 1954), p. 40.
2. Lazo, *La teoría*, p. 40.
3. Salvador Bueno, "La literatura cubana de la República," in *Medio siglo de literatura cubana* (Havana, 1953), p. 23.
4. Lazo, *La teoría*, p. 43.
5. Bueno, "La literatura," in *Medio siglo*, p. 24.
6. José Juan Arrom, *Esquema generacional de las letras* (Bogotá, 1963), p. 19.
7. Bueno, "Medio siglo de literatura narrativa," in *Medio siglo*, pp. 70–79, 82–83.
8. Félix Soloni, *Mersé* (Havana, 1926), p. 6. Subsequent references to this work will be made parenthetically in the text.
9. Enrique Anderson-Imbert and Lawrence B. Kiddle, *Veinte cuentos hispanoamericanos del siglo veinte* (New York, 1956).

10. José A. Portuondo, *Bosquejo histórico de las letras cubanas* (Havana, 1960), p. 62.
11. Lino Novás Calvo, *El negrero* (Madrid, 1955), p. 32. Subsequent references to this work will be made parenthetically in the text.
12. See Portuondo, *Bosquejo*, p. 61; Salvador Bueno, *Antología del cuento en Cuba (1902–1952)* (Havana, 1953), p. 233, and "Semblanza crítica de un narrador," in *Medio siglo*, p. 231.
13. Anderson-Imbert and Kiddle, *Veinte cuentos*, p. 133.
14. Portuondo, *Bosquejo*, p. 61.
15. Bueno, "Semblanza crítica," in *Medio siglo*, p. 220.
16. José Antonio Ramos, *Caniquí* (Havana, 1963), p. 8. Subsequent references to this work will be made parenthetically in the text.
17. Juan J. Remos y Rubio, "En torno a José Antonio Ramos y su labor como novelista," *Revista iberoamericana* 12 (June 1947): 287.
18. José Antonio Portuondo, "El contenido político y social de las obras de José Antonio Ramos," *Revista iberoamericana* 12 (June 1947): 242.
19. John E. Englekirk, "Caniquí," *Revista hispánica moderna* 3 (April 1937): 222.
20. Fernando Algería, *Historia de la novela hispanoamericana* (Mexico, 1965), p. 275.
21. Alejo Carpentier, *Tientos y diferencias* (Montevideo, 1967), pp. 10–11.
22. Alejo Carpentier, "Confesiones sencillas de un escritor barroco," *Cuba* 3, no. 24 (April 1964): 33; also quoted by Klaus Müller-Bergh, "Alejo Carpentier," *Revista iberoamericana* 33 (January–June 1967): 27–28.
23. Carpentier, "Problemática," in *Tientos*, p. 20.
24. Carpentier, "Confesiones sencillas," p. 32.
25. Müller-Bergh, "Alejo Carpentier," p. 30.
26. Alejo Carpentier, *El reino de este mundo* (Santiago, Chile, 1967), pp. 12, 14.
27. See Arrom, *Esquema*, pp. 194–213; Lazo, *La teoría*, pp. 43–44; Bueno, "La literatura," in *Medio siglo*, pp. 24–25.
28. *Américas* 2 (March 1950): 21–22; also quoted by Müller-Bergh, "Alejo Carpentier," p. 14.
29. Alejo Carpentier, *La música en Cuba* (Mexico, 1946), p. 236; also quoted by Müller-Bergh, "Alejo Carpentier," pp. 14–15.
30. Alejo Carpentier, *¡Ecue-Yamba-O!* (Madrid, 1933), p. 225. Subsequent references to this work will be made parenthetically in the text.
31. Carpentier, "Confesiones sencillas," p. 31.
32. Alegría, *Historia*, p. 277.
33. Müller-Bergh, "Alejo Carpentier," p. 26.
34. Carpentier, "Confesiones sencillas," p. 32.
35. Carpentier, *Tientos*, pp. 11–12; also quoted by Müller-Bergh, "Alejo Carpentier," p. 26.
36. Alegría, *Historia*, p. 277.
37. Ibid., p. 217.
38. Müller-Bergh, "Alejo Carpentier," p. 30.

39. Bueno, "Medio siglo de literatura narrativa," in *Medio siglo*, p. 83.
40. Carpentier, *El reino*, p. 16. Subsequent references to this work will be made parenthetically in the text.
41. Salvador Bueno, "Alejo Carpentier, novelista antillano y universal," in *La letra como testigo* (Las Villas, Cuba, 1957), p. 168; also quoted by Müller-Bergh, "Alejo Carpentier," p. 32.
42. Alegría, *Historia*, p. 278.
43. Ibid.

Bibliography

Alegría, Fernando. *Historia de la novela hispanoamericana.* Mexico, 1965.

Alfonso, Paco. *Yari-Yari, mamá Olúa.* Havana, 1941.

Anderson-Imbert, Enrique. *Historia de la literatura hispanoamericana.* 2 vols. Mexico, 1962.

Anderson-Imbert, Enrique, and Kiddle, Lawrence B. *Veinte cuentos hispanoamericanos del siglo veinte.* New York, 1956.

Arredondo, Alberto. *El negro en Cuba.* Havana, 1939.

Arrom, José Juan. *Esquema generacional de las letras hispanoamericanas.* Bogotá, 1963.

————. *Historia de la literatura dramática cubana.* New Haven, 1944.

————. "La poesía afrocubana." In *Estudios de literatura hispanoamericana.* Havana, 1950.

————. "Presencia del negro en la poesía folklórica americana." In *Miscelánea de estudios dedicados a Fernando Ortiz.* Havana, 1955.

————. "El teatro de José Antonio Ramos." *Revista iberoamericana* 12 (June 1947): 263–71.

Balboa, Silvestre de. *Espejo de paciencia.* Edited by Cintio Vitier. Las Villas, Cuba, 1960.

Ballagas, Emilio. *Mapa de la poesía negra americana.* Buenos Aires, 1946.

Bueno, Salvador. "Alejo Carpentier, novelista antillano y universal." In *La letra como testigo.* Las Villas, Cuba, 1957.

————. *Antología del cuento en Cuba (1902–1952).* Havana, 1953.

————. *Medio siglo de literatura cubana.* Havana, 1953.

————. "La literatura cubana de la República." In *Medio siglo.*

————. "Medio siglo de literatura narrativa. In *Medio Siglo.*

Cabrera Saqui, Mario. "Vida, pasión, y gloria de Anselmo Suárez y Romero." In *Francisco* by Anselmo Suárez y Romero. Havana, 1947.

Calcagno, Francisco. *Aponte.* Barcelona, 1901.

————. *Poetas de color.* Havana, 1878.

——. *Romualdo: Uno de tantos.* Havana, 1891.

Carbonell, José Manuel. *Evolución de la cultura cubana: La prosa en Cuba.* Vol. 12, book 2. Havana, 1928.

Carpentier, Alejo. "Confesiones sencillas de un escritor barroco." *Cuba* 3, no. 24 (April 1964): 30–33.

——. *¡Ecué-Yamba-O!* Madrid, 1933.

——. *La música en Cuba.* Mexico, 1946.

——. "Problemática de la actual novela latinoamericana." In *Tientos y diferencias.* Montevideo, 1967.

——. *El reino de este mundo.* Santiago, Chile, 1967.

——. "Variaciones sobre un tema cubano." *Américas* 2, no. 3 (March 1950): 21–22.

Chacon y Calvo, José María. *Las cien mejores poesías cubanas.* Madrid, 1922.

Coello, Francisco. *Atlas de España y sus posesiones de ultramar,* s.v. "Cuba." Madrid, 1851.

Cotarelo y Mori, Emilio. *La Avellaneda y sus obras.* Madrid, 1930.

Coulthard, G. R. *Raza y color en la literatura antillana.* Seville, 1958.

Cruz, Manuel de la. *Cromitos cubanos. Obras completas,* vol. 5. Madrid, 1926.

——. "Antonio Zambrana." In *Cromitos cubanos.*

——. "Cirilo Villaverde." In *Cromitos cubanos.*

——. "Francisco Calcagno." In *Cromitos cubanos.*

——. "Ramón Meza." In *Cromitos cubanos.*

——. "Cecilia Valdés." In *Literatura cubana. Obras completas,* vol. 3. Madrid, 1926.

Englekirk, John E. "Caniquí." *Revista hispánica moderna* 3 (April 1937): 222–23.

Escarpenter, José Antonio. "Presentación." In *Panorama histórico del teatro cubano.* Havana, 1965.

Fernández Retamar, Roberto. *La poesia contemporánea en Cuba (1927–1953).* Havana, 1954.

Figarola-Caneda, Domingo. *Gertrudis Gómez de Avellaneda.* Madrid, 1929.

Flores, Angel. "Magical Realism in Spanish American Fiction." *Hispania* 38 (1955): 187–92.

Ford, Jeremiah D. *A Bibliography of Cuban Belles-Lettres.* Cambridge, 1933.

Franco, José Luciano. "Estudio preliminar." In *Autobiografía, versos y cartas* by Juan Francisco Manzano. Havana, 1937.

García Vega, Lorenzo. *Antología de la novela cubana.* Havana, 1960.

Gómez de Avellaneda, Gertrudis. *Autobiografía y cartas.* Edited by Lorenzo Cruz de Fuentes. Huelva, 1907.

——. *Sab.* 2 vols. Madrid, 1841.

González Freire, Natividad. *Teatro cubano 1927–1961.* Havana, 1961.

Guerra, Ramiro. *Manual de historia de Cuba.* Havana, 1962.

Guirao, Ramón. *Orbita de la poesía afrocubana.* Havana, 1938.

Henríquez Ureña, Max. *Panorama histórico de la literatura cubana.* 2 vols. New York, 1963.

Henríquez Ureña, Pedro. *Las corrientes literaias en la América hispana.* Mexico, 1949.

Homenaje a Cirilo Villaverde. Havana, 1964.

Humboldt, Alejandro de. *Ensayo político sobre la isla de Cuba.* 2 vols. Havana, 1930.

Jackson, Richard L. "Miscegenation and Personal Choice in Two Twentieth-Century Novels of Continental Spanish America." *Hispana* 1 (1967): 86–88.

Lazo, Raimundo. *La teoría de las generaciones y su aplicación al estudio histórico de la literatura cubana.* Havana, 1954.

Lizaso, Félix. *Ensayistas contemporáneos.* Havana, 1938.

López Prieto, Antonio. *Parnaso cubano.* Havana, 1881.

Manzano, Juan Francisco. *Autobiografía, versos y cartas.* Havana, 1937.

Martí, José. *Obras completas.* 2 vols. Havana, 1946.

Menton, Seymour. "In Search of a Nation." *Hispania* 38 (1955): 432–42.

Meza, Ramón. *Carmela.* Havana, 1887.

Milanés, José Jacinto. *Obras completas.* Havana, 1920.

Mitjans, Aurelio. *Estudio sobre el movimiento científico y literario de Cuba.* Havana, 1963.

Monte, Domingo del. *Centón epistolario.* 7 vols. Havana, 1926–57.

Morales y Morales, Vidal. *Iniciadores y primeros mártires de la revolución cubana.* 4 vols. Havana, 1931.

Morúa Delgado, Martín. *Impresiones literarias: Las novelas del señor Villaverde.* Havana, 1892.

————. *Sofía.* Havana, 1891.

Müller-Bergh, Klaus, "Alejo Carpentier: Autor y obra en su época." *Revista iberoamericana* 33 (January–June 1967): 9–43.

Novás Calvo, Lino. *El negrero.* Madrid, 1955.

Nunn, Marshall E. "Some Notes on the Cuban Novel *Cecilia Valdés.*" *Bulletin of Hispanic Studies* 24 (1947): 184–86.

Olivera, Otto. *Breve historia de la literatura antillana.* Mexico, 1957.

Ortiz, Fernando. *La antigua fiesta afrocubana del "Día de Reyes."* Havana, 1960.

————. *Los negros brujos.* Madrid, n.d.

————. *Los negros esclavos.* Havana, 1916.

Panorama del teatro cubano. Havana, 1965.

Peraza Sarausa, Fermín. *Anuario bibliográfico cubano.* Havana, 1937–59; Miami, 1959–69.

————. "Bibliografía de José Antonio Ramos." *Revista iberoamericana* 12 (June 1947): 335–400.

Percas Ponseti, Helena. "Sobre la Avellaneda y su novela *Sab.*" *Revista iberoamericana* 38 (1962): 347–57.

Portuondo, José Antonio. *Bosquejo histórico de las letras cubanas.* Havana, 1960.

————. "El contenido político y social de las obras de José Antonio Ramos." *Revista iberoamericana* 12 (June 1947): 215–50.

Rabassa, Gregory. *The Negro in Brazilian Fiction since 1888.* New York, 1954.

Ramos, José Antonio. *Caniquí.* Havana, 1963.

Remos y Rubio, Juan J. *Historia de la literatura cubana.* 3 vols. Havana, 1945.

————. *Tendencias de la narración imaginativa en Cuba.* Havana, 1935.

————. "En torno a José Antonio Ramos y su labor como novelista." *Revista iberoamericana* 12 (June 1947): 279–89.

Roig de Leuchsenring, Emilio. *La Habana, apuntes históricos.* 3 vols. Havana, 1963.

Rosenblat, Angel. *El mestizaje y las castas coloniales.* Buenos Aires, 1954.

————. *La población indígena (1942–1950).* Buenos Aires, 1954.

Saco, José Antonio. *Historia de la esclavitud.* 4 vols. Paris, 1975.

————. *Papeles sobre Cuba.* Havana, 1960.

Santovenia, Emeterio S. and Shelton, Raúl M. *Cuba y su historia.* 3 vols. Miami, 1965.

Sayers, Raymond S. *The Negro in Brazilian Literature.* New York, 1956.

Soloni, Félix. *Mersé.* Havana, 1926.

Suárez-Murias, Marguerite C. *La novela romántica en Hispanoamérica.* New York, 1963.

Suárez y Romero, Anselmo. *Francisco: El ingenio; o, Las delicias del campo.* Havana, 1947.

Tanco y Bosmoniel, Félix M. *Petrano y Rosalía. Cuba contemporánea* 39 (December 1925): 255–88.

Tejera, Diego Vicente. "Una novela cubana." In *Un poco de prosa.* Havana, 1895.

Torriente, Loló de la. *La Habana de Cecilia Valdés.* Havana, 1946.

Trelles, Carlos M. *Bibliografía cubana de los siglos XVII y XVIII.* Havana, 1927.

————. *Bibliografía cubana del siglo XIX.* 7 vols. Matanzas, Cuba, 1911–14.

————. *Bibliografía cubana del siglo XX.* 2 vols. Matanzas, Cuba, 1916–17.

Varona, Enrique José. "El autor de *Cecilia Valdés.*" In *Homenaje a Cirilo Villaverde.* Havana, 1964.

Villaverde, Cirilo. *Cecilia Valdés* Edited by Olga Blondet Tudisco and Antonio Tudisco. New York, 1964.

Vitier, Cintio. *Cincuenta años de poesía cubana.* Havana, 1952.

Zambrana y Vázquez, Antonio. *El negro Francisco.* Havana, 1948.

Zum Felde, Alberto. *Indice crítico de la literatura hispanoamericana: La narrativa.* Mexico, 1959.

Index

Library of Congress Cataloging in Publication Data
Barreda, Pedro, 1933–
The Black protagonist in the Cuban novel.
Translation of La caracterización del protagonista
negro en la novela cubana.
Bibliography: p.
1. Cuban fiction—History and criticism.   2. Blacks
in literature.   I.   Title.
PQ7382.B313   863   78-19689
ISBN 0-87023-262-2